ABRAHAM LINCOLN

AND THE AMERICAN POLITICAL TRADITION

ABRAHAM ⋆ LINCOLN

and the American Political Tradition

EDITED BY JOHN L. THOMAS

The University of Massachusetts Press

Amherst, 1986

Set in Linoterm Bembo at The University of Massachusetts Press
Printed by Cushing-Malloy, Inc. and bound by John H. Dekker & Sons
Library of Congress Cataloging-in-Publication Data
Main entry under title:
Abraham Lincoln and the American political tradition.
"The essays in this volume were presented in
briefer form as papers at a conference on "Lincoln and
the American Political Tradition" held at Brown
University, June 7–9, 1984, and sponsored by the
university's John Hay Library and the Lincoln Group
of Boston"—Acknowledgments.
1. Lincoln, Abraham, 1809–1865—Addresses, essays,
lectures. 2. United States—Politics and government—
1849–1877—Addresses, essays, lectures. I. Thomas,
John L. II. Brown University. Library. III. Lincoln
Group of Boston.
E457.8.A239   1986   973.7   85–20973
ISBN 0–87023–512–5 (alk. paper)

Frontispiece: Lincoln in the House of Representatives, February 25, 1861.
Pencil and wash drawing by Thomas Nast. The printed version appeared
in the *New York Illustrated News,* March 16, 1861. The drawing, taken
from Nast's Civil War scrapbook, is published here for the first time.
Courtesy McLellan Lincoln Collection, John Hay Library,
Brown University.

ACKNOWLEDGMENTS

THE ESSAYS IN THIS VOLUME WERE PRESENTED IN BRIEFER form as papers at a conference on "Lincoln and the American Political Tradition" held at Brown University, June 7–9, 1984, and sponsored by the university's John Hay Library and The Lincoln Group of Boston. The editor is indebted to the three commentators at the sessions—Robert V. Bruce of Boston University, Richard N. Current, Distinguished Professor of History Emeritus, University of North Carolina at Greensboro, and Gordon S. Wood of Brown University—for their criticism and comments, of which, they will note, he has made full use. Thanks are also due to Samuel A. Streit, Assistant University Librarian for Special Collections at Brown, Jennifer B. Lee of the John Hay Library, and Frank J. Williams, president of The Lincoln Group of Boston and chair, Lincoln Advisory Committee, Brown University, for planning the conference and providing invaluable logistical and editorial help.

CONTENTS

ABRAHAM LINCOLN

AND THE AMERICAN POLITICAL TRADITION

JOHN L. THOMAS

★

Introduction

ABRAHAM LINCOLN WAS SHAPED BY THE DEMOCRATIC FORCES
of the age in which he lived and, in turn, gave enduring form to its politics, which is to say that Lincoln inherited a political culture and fashioned from it a national liberal tradition. For Americans who came to
maturity in the Age of Jackson the recent achievement of independence
and nationhood provided a storehouse of memories, models, and pre-
cepts. The great work of the founding fathers embodied in their documents—the Declaration of Independence and the Constitution—retained an immediacy of example undiminished by the passing of half
a century. Lincoln's cohort of rising young politicians held the collective image of the founders constantly before them as both lesson and
challenge. Lincoln spoke for this generation in his address to the Young
Men's Lyceum in Springfield in 1838 in reminding his listeners of the
"legacy bequeathed us by a once hardy, brave, and patriotic, but now
lamented and departed, race of ancestors." Theirs had been the task of
building "a political edifice of liberty and equal rights." His own age,
Lincoln concluded, now faced the "task of gratitude to our fathers, justice to ourselves, duty to posterity, and love for our species in general."

Lincoln, like his political comrades, championed the cause of the
new cultural figure so appealing to a romantic age—the hero in history endowed with a consciousness of his world-historical role and
equipped with the ambition, energy, and will to fulfill it. As he ex-

3

plained, "Towering genius disdains a beaten path. It seeks regions hitherto unexplored." The original accomplishments of the founders and the dedication of their sons to spreading the democratic example across the world seemed to Lincoln and his generation the unfolding of a providential plan and proof of their redemptive destiny.

If these articles of political faith clustered at the center of the antebellum American consciousness, along the edges of the popular mind lay other more homely images and themes which Lincoln also appropriated for his purposes: the advantages of a humble origin and the certain rise from obscurity in a land of opportunity; the virtue of a life lived close to the soil by nature's noblemen; the vision of a limitless West with its promise of a second chance. And the hovering presence of divine purpose manifested in visions and dreams, visitations and afflictions, signs and portents—a rich lore of democratic popular culture. The search for the political culture from which Lincoln emerged leads out of the halls of state and into the American heartland of popular assumptions and aspirations where programs give way to persuasions, platforms to preferences, ideology to *mentalité*. Yet tracing the process by which Lincoln molded this cultural material into a new doctrine of liberal nationalism involves a return to the political center and to the politics of slavery, union, and civil war.

The essays in this volume view Lincoln as both giver and receiver— as initially bound by the expectations and constraints of Jacksonian society but as finally transcending them. In the opening essay, "Lincoln's Fraternal Democracy," Robert H. Wiebe describes these new social forces and democratic ideals that were the "common cultural property" of Jacksonian Americans and that determined the outlook of Lincoln and his cohort of young men-on-the-make in a disordered world of great expectations. Wiebe depicts the democratic society fashioned by the American Revolution and subsequent religious revivals as contemptuous of all inherited social distinctions and hierarchical arrangements yet at the same time in desperate need of new gradations and lines of demarcation. These he proceeds to draw as the boundaries of Lincoln's midwestern world which served as a cultural fence for his political ambitions. One of the most clearly recognizable divisions in antebellum America was that between the sexes, a line separating politics as a man's world from culture as the genteel province of women. Lincoln, according to Wiebe, flourished in this world divided between cracker barrels and front parlors by opting to become and remain a "man's man"—distinctly uncomfortable in the presence of the opposite sex and happiest among his cronies whose practice of male bonding testified to the stifling atmosphere of the cult of gentility. "Lincoln's democracy," Wiebe writes, "was a fraternity, rooted in the man's world of law and politics and then extended nationwide." If Lincoln and his fraternity brothers managed to escape the confines of an official domesticity, so too, it should be noted, did an increasing number of restive and reform-minded women who abandoned the code of hearth and husbandly guiding hand for new forms of sisterhood and liberation. But it was Lincoln's peculiarly intense feelings of political comradeship, Wiebe argues, that was the source of the great compassion which contemporaries of both sexes recognized and which subsequently became the stuff of legend. When the Civil War came and he was forced to send hundreds of thousands of young men to the slaughterbench, Lincoln's deeply held values of fraternity and equality "stiffened" his resolve but also "wrung his heart." "In this great fraternity of equals," Wiebe concludes, "he and they belonged together."

Political culture in the Age of Jackson was vigorously rhetorical. In "The Words of Lincoln" Don E. Fehrenbacher analyzes Lincoln's mastery of the written and spoken word, and at the same time points to the difficulties confronting the historian who seeks to authenticate that word. An appreciation of Lincoln's political language, Fehrenbacher suggests, involves a certainty as to its provenance, a clear sense of the relevant audience, an understanding of political strategy, but above all, a susceptibility to the sheer power of language. For Wiebe, the words of Lincoln's fraternity constitute a functional glossary and define a popular style. For Fehrenbacher, Lincoln's own words at their most compelling become forms of moral action.

In providing a few "cautionary rules" for quoting Lincoln, Fehrenbacher reminds us that maximum accuracy is no mere "pedantic ideal" but an absolute necessity. He proceeds to apply all his strictures in examining several Lincoln texts, chief among them the House Divided speech and what might be called "The Case of the Misplaced Transposition," which he solves with a bit of literary detective work. Significant interpretation, Fehrenbacher argues, ultimately means distinguishing between intentional, consequential, and transcendent meaning, the first involving a sensitivity to the often close political calculations of Lincoln, the second a familiarity with his political setting, and the third a sound knowledge of the canons of political rhetoric. "Lincoln's literary skill," Fehrenbacher concludes, "is perhaps most open to view in those instances when he took someone else's prose and molded it to his own use." It is on this highest level of transcendent meaning that an unformed political culture suddenly and mysteriously hardens into tradition, and eloquence becomes a political act. The compassion that Wiebe derives from Lincoln's sense of comradeship has been elevated through Lincoln's mastery of langauge to a universal appeal.

In "Who Voted for Lincoln?" William E. Gienapp turns from Lincoln the presidential aspirant to the voters who elected him. In Gienapp's essay Lincoln retires behind a screen of carefully collated election statistics for nine northern states in the election of 1860. The voting patterns that Gienapp uncovers provide evidence for a number of generalizations, some of them confirming long-held impressions of Republican strength, others pointing to heretofore unrecognized factors that account for Republican victory. While it is not surprising to learn that Lincoln did better among rural than urban voters, proved stronger with Protestants than Catholics, and held more appeal for skilled than unskilled workers, Gienapp's data and analysis underscore the diversity of voter response to the party and its candidate. Maine farmers, for example, strongly supported the Lincoln ticket while Iowa farmers did not. Religious preference, even among Protestants, dictated quite different political choices, and nowhere did wealth alone determine the outcome.

Gienapp's findings also call attention to two significant factors, both previously ignored, which account for Lincoln's victory. The first of these is the marked success of Republicans in turning out the youth vote. Republican Wide Awake societies modeled on earlier Know-Nothing marching organizations were composed overwhelmingly of young men. "Donning a uniform of glazed caps and oil-cloth capes and carrying torches attached to a rail, members marched . . . in military-like drill, chanting slogans, singing campaign songs, and cheering the party's candidates." Suddenly politicized by shrewd Republican managers, Wide-Awakes supplied the partisan spirit and raucous tone of the campaign and in doubtful states helped tip the balance toward Lincoln.

The second major conclusion that Gienapp draws from his data is that Republican victory was fashioned in large measure from the votes of defecting Know-Nothings who had voted for Fillmore four years earlier. Although Lincoln voters comprised a broad coalition, "finally," Gienapp concludes, "the overwhelming backing Lincoln won among former Know-Nothings was perhaps the most important shift that produced his victory." Still, the composite picture that Gienapp draws suggests a wide variety of economic interests, ethnic origins, religious preferences, and moral stances. Gienapp's essay raises crucial questions as to the original Republican contribution to the American political tradition. What were Lincoln's own political leanings? How important was his Whig background in determining his ideas of party and presidential office? What happened to the broad coalition of Republican interest groups under the hammerings of a four-year war? And finally, how did Lincoln actually harmonize these various collisive factions within the party? If, in short, elections provide the acid test for political traditions, what was the tradition out of which Lincoln came, and did he follow, revise, or abandon it in prosecuting the war?

In the next two essays Stephen B. Oates and Michael F. Holt offer dramatically different answers to these and other questions. Proceeding from similar revisionist points of departure, they reach opposite conclusions as to the precise nature of Lincoln's contribution to the American political tradition. In "Abraham Lincoln: *Republican* in the White House," Oates questions and then rejects the argument advanced by David Donald in his highly influential essay, "Abraham Lincoln: Whig in the White House," that Lincoln remained captive to the Whig tradition of a limited presidency. Donald points to the "peculiar paradox" of a strong executive wielding the war power with an energy bordering on ruthlessness who was at the same time strangely reluctant to employ similar force in pursuing a domestic policy and directing Congress in implementing it. Lincoln's hesitation Donald attributes to his Whig heritage and a view of the presidential office as primarily facilitative.

It is this assessment of Lincoln's divided mind that Oates challenges. Lincoln, he insists, was confronted by a crisis of unprecedented proportions for which no political leader could have been prepared. Once in office, he quickly realized the enormity of his task and set about the work of building a war machine, rallying his party, tightening his administration, prodding a laggard Congress, and slowly but inexorably moving the issue of slavery to the center of northern consciousness.

Lincoln, as Oates presents him, was first and last a Republican who subscribed to the doctrine of free labor and free soil, taught soldier and civilian alike the meaning of national union, and, defying public opinion, issued the Emancipation Proclamation—"the most revolutionary measure to come from an American president up to that time." Whatever his initial reservations, Lincoln assumed leadership of a "remorseless revolutionary struggle." His response to the war "defined him as president" in a way that neither he nor anyone else could have predicted: leader of a new and vital party; architect of a national policy; prophet of a new moral politics; master builder of the American political tradition. Oates thus offers a psychological portrait of a paragon of the self-made man—the ambitious politician who by a heroic act of will made himself over into a great statesman.

In "Abraham Lincoln and the Politics of Union," Michael F. Holt presents a view of Lincoln the president and party leader at wide variance from Oates's. Holt also begins by reassessing a long-accepted thesis, this one argued by Eric McKitrick in an original essay, "Party Politics and the Union and Confederate War Efforts," in which he attributes the successful prosecution of the war by Lincoln's government in large part to the existence of a vital two-party system in the North, which the Confederacy lacked. The oppositional stance of the Democratic party throughout the war, according to McKitrick, forced Republicans to assume a posture of unity, sharpened their partisan skills, clarified their program for carrying on the war, and thus, however unintentionally, contributed to the winning of the war.

Holt, in inverting the McKitrick thesis, gives an account of Lincoln's wartime political aims and strategies which differs substantially from Oates's estimate. In the first place, Holt sees Lincoln's Whig origins as a continuing source of his political behavior. All Lincoln's Whig predecessors—Tyler, Taylor, and Fillmore—had attempted to convert a narrowly based political organization into a broad party of national union. Lincoln, in his turn and for reasons of principle as well as expediency, sought to follow their example in a series of wartime political maneuvers that alienated the fiercely partisan congressional wing of the Republican party. Where Oates presents Lincoln as a supremely successful leader of his party—"a principled and dedicated Republican" who adroitly managed his congressional opposition—Holt emphasizes the sharp conflicts between president and Republican congressmen, each with separate constituencies, political strategies, and war aims. Moreover, it was no mere redistribution of power within his party that Lincoln sought. "This was *not* simply a matter of broadening the base of the Republican party as some historians have maintained," explains Holt. "Rather it was an attempt to replace the Republican party with a new bisectional organization to be called the Union party. . . . To state the argument most boldly, Lincoln . . . set out to destroy the Republican party as it existed in 1860, that is, as an exclusively northern party whose sole basis of cohesion was hostility toward the South and the Democratic party."

Congressional Republicans grew increasingly hostile to Lincoln's large policy and soon were opposing his scheme at every step. When the border states refused to consider Lincoln's plan for the gradual elimination of slavery and northern Democrats declined the proffered presidential hand, hopes for an intersectional party of all talents dimmed, and it was left to the hapless Andrew Johnson to take up the dwindling option. Yet the attempted reconstruction of his party, Holt argues, is proof of Lincoln's pragmatic reading of the American political tradition as a balance between principles and expediency. If Gienapp discovers the traces of a political tradition in the voting patterns and Oates discerns it in the forging of a presidential will, Holt finds the essential Lincoln in the political sagacity of a modern president who knew that the first rule of politics is to win office and hold on to it.

In the final essay in this collection, "Abraham Lincoln and the Second American Revolution," James M. McPherson draws on the sources afforded by both political culture and political tradition. In the center of the collective American consciousness in the years before the Civil War lay memories of the recent American Revolution and the lessons it presumably had taught to a chosen people. The Revolution supplied the articles of a secular faith complete with sacred text, saints and martyrs, and a redemptive mission. But the political culture bequeathed to Jacksonian Americans by the first American Revolution also contained fundamental contradictions which, as McPherson points out, Lincoln and his generation attempted to resolve by making a second American Revolution.

The Civil War, in McPherson's view, can be considered a revolution in three ways. In the first place, the Confederates invoked the right of revolution proclaimed in the Declaration of Independence, and in seceding from the Union sought to make "a revolution in behalf of the liberty to preserve slavery." In flatly rejecting this appeal, Lincoln reminded the secessionists that "we all declare for liberty; but in using the same *word* we do not all mean the same thing." Studying the language of the Declaration and the several secession ordinances with the care that Fehrenbacher now urges on historians, Lincoln based his rejection of the southern appeal to the right of revolution on the phrase "for just cause," which, he insisted, was precisely what the Confederacy lacked.

While Lincoln denied the right of secession and thus proclaimed himself a counterrevolutionary, he willingly embraced the second principle of the American Revolution—the equality of peoples—and in this sense completed the revolutionary work of the founders. In carrying out their mandate, McPherson explains, Lincoln was a "conservative revolutionary" unconvinced of racial equality but determined to destroy slavery. And once it was clear to him that compromise and conciliation had failed, he became the most thoroughgoing of revolutionaries in a third sense by making a social revolution that abolished slavery, uprooted southern institutions, and overturned the balance of power and wealth between North and South. Unlike Robespierre or Lenin, Lincoln was not an ideological but a pragmatic revolutionary driven by the exigencies of war to identify equality with preserving the Union. "It was *the war itself*," concludes McPherson, "not the ideological blueprints of Lincoln or any other leader, that generated the radical momentum that made it a second American Revolution."

In these essays Lincoln appears in several guises: as the ambitious member of a political fraternity; as a master of political discourse; as an able tactician and party leader; as an embattled executive; and as a committed if conservative revolutionary. Yet in all of these postures he may be seen collecting the raw materials afforded by an emergent national culture and forging from them his own vision of liberty and union.

ROBERT H. WIEBE

★

Lincoln's Fraternal Democracy

UNIQUE AMONG THE GREAT AMERICAN PRESIDENTS, ABRAHAM
Lincoln enters our consciousness through the emotions. As school
children we are taught to love him for the love he gave his own children, for the sympathy he revealed in his wartime pardons, for the pain
he suffered from the terrible battlefield slaughter. When we are told that
Lincoln could not finish a favorite poem because its last lines choked
him with anguish for the wartime dead, our hearts go with him. The
best of the Lincoln statuary plays on this same image of soulful sadness:
the head bowed, the thoughts enveloping a leader who endures the nation's crisis though his heart is breaking. Even the tough-minded,
myth-shattering scholars of the mid-twentieth century who have given
us Lincoln the politically seasoned Whig on the make leave a good deal
of this tormented older man intact. Can we imagine tears for the dead
from Franklin Roosevelt or Woodrow Wilson or George Washington?
A distinguishably Lincolnian quality requires an explanation. "With
malice toward none, with charity for all. . . ." Listening to Lincoln
deliver those lines, Walt Whitman heard a singular mix of "tenderness"
and "manliness," and in a very general way, Whitman's observation
serves as the theme of this essay.

Whence came Lincoln's particular kind of compassion? Our best approach to the problem takes us to the culture surrounding him. What
would be a sensible strategy in any case becomes almost mandatory in

Lincoln's for reasons of evidence alone. With only fragments of information about his first twenty years and little more than scraps about his next ten, we encounter a mature Lincoln before we have access to a substantial body of material about him. Unable to follow him upward from birth, we are obliged to pursue the grown man outward. How did the adult Lincoln make use of a common cultural property? In general, personality and culture fitted nicely, but on two important matters—equality and fraternity—Lincoln clearly stretched what was available to suit himself. An understanding of the Lincolnian difference begins with an exploration of these subjects.

LINCOLN, born in 1809, came of age in the 1820s as Americans were self-consciously fashioning a democratic society. No problem bedeviled this new society more persistently or touched a wider range of its public issues than the challenge of making useful, justifiable distinctions inside a polity that resonated with the praises of equality. Its predecessor, the society of the revolutionary era, had taken for granted numerous superior-inferior relations—in personal dealings, social privileges, constitutional powers, and public life generally. Assuming the inevitability of such distinctions, leaders in the late eighteenth century had struggled to create the right ones in principle while tolerating a good deal of blurring in the particulars. An adaptable interior design of many, misty gradations enabled the gentry society of Jefferson and Hamilton to survive revolution and remain to be reckoned with at the beginning of the nineteenth century.

During Lincoln's teenage years, agents of democracy throughout the United States set about eliminating the last of these inequalities, and at least as public standards the shaded tiers of the eighteenth century disappeared. Lincoln's cohort, inheriting a flattened egalitarianism, also acquired the task of reorganizing the interior of this leveled society. Between the 1820s and the 1850s, Americans characteristically replaced the old multitude of imprecise gradations with a few boldly drawn lines of separation. The best remembered of these, a line through the Louisiana Purchase at 36°30' and, by extension eastward, across the full breadth of the United States, divided free soil from slave. Where a line was the norm, its absence was the unsettling alternative, as the Wilmot Proviso demonstrated in the late forties and the repeal of the Missouri Compromise line in the Nebraska Territory demonstrated in the mid-fifties. In each instance the opponents of these measures fell naturally into the role of the aggrieved party, arguing from the assumption that a clear line for expansion was something close to an American's civil right, and a number of compromise solutions between 1848 and 1861 relied on this faith in the magical efficacy of the right line to solve America's problems. By the late fifties, however, fears were chronic that not even the most basic lines held any longer in American society, conjuring among moderate Northerners a vision of an enveloping Slave Power and among moderate Southerners the specter of imperial abolitionism. Lincoln's law partner William Herndon, expressing the customary wisdom about such formless, overlapping competition, wrote in 1856: "Freedom or slavery . . . must perish quickly."[1]

The constitutionalism that underlay public policy relied just as heavily on a sense of clear, firm lines. As the pioneers of democracy flattened their society early in the nineteenth century, they also destroyed the hierarchical model of American government that had enabled its founders to picture local, state, and national levels within an integrated whole. The most zealous eighteenth-century republicans, who guarded against every hint of "consolidation" and resisted every additional power for a national government, had still acknowledged the superior place of the Constitution's "general government": it stood above the other levels. Now all governments occupied the same plane, and in one of the great obsessions of the nineteenth century, Americans argued ceaselessly about the lines dividing those governments from one another. By and large, they debated as local citizens. When even a notably ambitious, well-informed Illinois Whig referred in 1844 to "the 'outer wall' of the [electoral] district," as if Vandals and Goths lay on the far side, he revealed the pervasiveness of American provincialism.[2] Beyond their localities, almost all Americans accepted the boundaries of the state as the impermeable markers of the nation's federalism. On the centrality of state sovereignty, if not on all of its implications, those who claimed to be followers of John C. Calhoun or Henry Clay or Andrew Jackson could agree.

National powers required a special justification, and by the 1840s party elders seldom felt inclined to mount one. "What would the Whigs have had the [national] Government to do?" an exasperated James K. Polk asked during the Panic of 1837. ". . . [W]hen whole classes, have contracted debts beyond their ability to meet, surely the Government is not answerable, because it possesses no power to restrain or permit it; nor can it pay their debts for them."³ Despite noises about a national bankruptcy law and a new national bank, Polk's views emerged as the consensus. By midcentury national statesmanship for Whigs and Democrats alike meant restraint, and leaders in both parties contrasted what irresponsible people wanted from the national government with the moderate, restricted range of what it could actually do.

The Constitution, the universal basis for these judgments, became the sole source for a whole America. Originally the Constitution had empowered a superior general government to preside at the top of the nation. Now that all governments sat side by side, only the Constitution itself girdled those governments into the United States. Americans debated the minutiae of constitutional doctrine not because they had a metaphysical bent or a love for learned disquisitions but because they had so much invested in those details. Constitutionalism was the glue for a nation. By enabling Americans to draw the essential lines of separation, the Constitution simultaneously created the bands that held the United States together.

Lincoln functioned comfortably within this configuration of lines. Where a strong line divided free from slave territory, he expressed considerable confidence in the ability of these contrary labor systems to live side by side. Where he found a blurred line, as under the Dred Scott decision, or no line at all, as under popular sovereignty, he anticipated deep troubles. Ambiguous boundaries invited the expansion of an aggrandizing Slave Power, and anyone who relied on the automatic workings of nature to protect the cause of free soil, Lincoln warned, was listening to a "lullaby." Nature helped those who helped themselves. Only by denying "new places for it to live in" would slavery die "a natural death."⁴ In addition to a line blocking slavery's growth, Lincoln committed himself just as firmly to a line preserving it inside those states where it existed. Local rights and state sovereignty had a concreteness in Lincoln's thinking that a distant national power could not match. When he proposed to rotate an Illinois congressional seat among one-term occupants during the 1840s, he followed a well-established custom of construing national office as a local reward. A similar spirit informed Lincoln's plan for the national government to sell land cheaply to the states so that the states could then sell it for their own profit.

At the same time, the American whole had a meaning to him that transcended a mere sum of these parts. The Constitution that fixed basic boundaries within the United States allowed this flat, delineated federalism to function at all, and as the adhesive for union it maintained democracy everywhere. "Truth is one . . . ," George Bancroft declared for American culture. "One truth cannot contradict another truth."[5] In Lincoln's scheme, the Constitution had sufficient importance to serve as a test for almost any other truth that might be set against it, a centrality that would warrant almost any sacrifice to preserve its unifying power.

Lincoln's linear constitutionalism sounded enough like that of Illinois Democrats and Whigs alike to locate him on the middle ground of his culture. His attitudes toward the new democracy's social structure, on the other hand, pushed him much closer to the edges of general agreement. As the levelers of the early nineteenth century erased their predecessors' many soft gradations, they placed the entire weight of their judgment on a single issue: in or out. Inside the egalitarian community, according to the norms of the new democracy, all men enjoyed access to the same social privileges and benefits. Hence the irrefutable contemporary logic that the mere entry of blacks into a white community would lead to "amalgamation." The one reliable protection against an irresistible equality was exclusion. By the 1820s, Americans were scrambling to th ν up new walls across the otherwise bare plains of their democracy. ιn succeeding decades the already grim lot of free blacks deteriorated further, and a multiplicity of theories from science, religion, and everyday prejudice justified the murder, enslavement, or ostracism of dark-skinned Americans. Various forms of collective violence underlined this message with a Jacksonian ferocity. During the forties and fifties, ethnic barriers also rose to bound the egalitarian world of white Protestants, as Catholics generally and the Irish in particular suffered harsher abuse, greater danger, and the growing prospect of civil disabilities. By the 1850s anti-Semitism was also sharpening. With additional bars against the propertyless and the transients, this division in its broadest sense marked a long class line across American society, welcoming about half the nation's population inside the new democracy and blocking the way for the other half.

These sensitivities deepened as Lincoln came of age, and the pattern of walls spread during his adult years. Although he never challenged the

core of his democratic society—the exclusionary, egalitarian community—he paid little attention to the paraphernalia of discriminations
that sustained it. Whenever Lincoln did confront one of these barriers,
however, he showed his distaste. He repudiated the anti-Catholic, anti-
Irish principles of the Know-Nothing party, which drew heavily from
his Whig associates. Indeed, Lincoln avoided the abuse of any group.
He opened a speech in September 1854 with a characteristic declaration
"that the Southern slaveholders were neither better, nor worse than we
of the North. . . . If we were situated as they are, we should act and feel
as they do; and if they were situated as we are, they should act and feel as
we do. . . ."[6] In 1858, when Stephen Douglas pressed him to extend
his remarks on the issue of black rights, he proposed a reasonably full
complement of them—compatible, that is, with the new democracy's
separation of the races. Over there, not here, blacks should have a
chance to pursue their opportunities. Granting blacks a narrower compass than whites seemed to grate on Lincoln, even though he almost
certainly thought of blacks as inferior. With a much simpler sweep of
judgment, he refused to proscribe poor whites. Certain retrospects on
Lincoln ring true: Frederick Douglass's, for example, that in personal
relations he was the least color-conscious public leader, and David
Davis's that as a lawyer "He never took advantage of a man's low character to prejudice the jury." "Lincoln seemed to put himself at once on
an equality with everybody," noted one of his law partners. "He was
always easy to approach and thoroughly democratic," commented
another.[7] Fittingly, Lincoln was that rare teetotaler who would not
condemn the heavy drinkers. By mid-nineteenth-century standards, in
sum, Lincoln showed a surprising lack of animus toward other people.

The diverging ways in which Lincoln and many of his contemporaries understood the meaning of the self-made man helped to illuminate the special cast of his democracy. As a conscious part of national
politics, the self-made man arrived with the presidential campaign of
1840, when the Whigs, under attack as elitists, used the concept to distinguish William Henry Harrison, their man of the people, from Martin
Van Buren, the scheming aristocrat. Four years later, Henry Clay, who
in 1832 had tried to cultivate the impression of a sophisticated alternative to the barbaric Jackson, allowed supporters to redesign his personal
history into that of a self-made man, and the major parties thereafter
vied with one another over the plainness of their candidates' origins and

the drama of their personal ascents. These images were then used in various ways to cover the new democracy's gaps in wealth and power.

The simplest application blended stories of the self-made man into the parties' promotional efforts to create an illusion of neighborly intimacy with their presidential aspirants: Old Rough, Young Hickory, Buck, Honest Abe. Candidates had been born just folks like the farmers and laborers who were being recruited to vote for them. In more complex ways, the self-made man served as a device to ease concerns among an upper class about its connections with a lower class. As Lincoln was entering politics, a gentleman in Tennessee decided "to test the question, whether a man could be elected without going among the people to electioneer. I quietly acquiesced" after a decisive defeat in 1833, he wrote, "and determined not to meddle with politics any more. . . ."[8] Such gentlemen with neither taste nor talent for campaigning across the class line counted on others to maintain communications with the poor. On the one hand, they ridiculed the results: "Wherever any man was found who could make a speech, or who thought he could make a speech, there a speech was made. . . ."[9] On the other hand, they prized those who could move across the divide with safe and sound messages for democracy's losers, binding haves and have-nots into one people with one government. No one seemed better suited for this unifying task than the self-made man, combining the instincts of his origins with the insights of his success, who could intuit the popular mind as he bent the popular ear.

Lincoln, praised by his Illinois contemporaries as an excellent stump speaker, was glorified at his death for a natural genius in tune with the people's simple wisdom. Herndon caught the essence of this myth in his summary of Lincoln the lawyer: "He knew nothing of the laws of evidence, of pleading, or of practice, and did not care about them; he had a keen sense of justice and struck for that, throwing aside forms, methods, and rules of all law."[10] But it was Joseph Gillespie, a politician with a strong sense of his own attachment to an Illinois elite, who better recognized the pacifying class effects—the surrogate triumph—of President Lincoln the self-made man: "The masses are naturally delighted at seeing one of their own class elevated . . . particularly if he succeeds by doing things in their way."[11]

The most obvious use of the self-made man as a sop to the poor came in the moralists' equation between an impoverished childhood and an adult strength of character. In this dispensation, poverty became a blessing, and a failure to rise above it lay exclusively with the individual. During the presidential campaign of 1860 the wealthy John Murray Forbes borrowed from this conception in his friendly description of Lincoln for an English acquaintance—"persistent and determined, half-educated, but self-reliant and self-taught."[12] After Lincoln's death, his Illinois associate Leonard Swett elaborated the image into a sketch of Lincoln's happy boyhood destitution. He would gladly have chosen to grow up in poverty, Swett concluded.

Lincoln, who had been living what others were transforming into a myth, had no liking for any of these variations on the self-made man. Campaign devices to disguise success and simulate a personal connection with the voters irritated him. He prided himself on the evidence of his rise to respectability, and he tolerated the promotional uses of "Abe" only because he could not change the rules of popular politics. Even then he refused to cooperate in claiming that he had once split rails. Though some Illinois Whigs who had never set eyes on Henry Clay called him "Harry of the West," Lincoln invariably referred to Clay in the same respectful terms that he wanted others to use toward him. No more a hair splitter than a rail splitter, Lincoln spoke and wrote simply because he believed in clarity, not because he was condescending to the uneducated. On the contrary, he paid his audiences the high compliment of assuming that any conscientious mind could comprehend the basics of any subject. Lincoln knew poverty intimately enough to hate it. He romanticized nothing about the body-breaking, spirit-crushing lives of the poor. Leaving poverty, not experiencing it, was the great victory, and he would have preferred not looking back at all. When he encouraged others to escape the same trap, Lincoln used the early nineteenth-century language of individual transcendence, a way of setting strength of character at odds with its environment: "if he *will*, he *can*."[13]

As a class division hardened around midcentury, successful Americans were promoting a myth of the self-made man to police its boundary line; but Lincoln, whose life was being fed into this myth, retained an earlier vision of the self-made man as his society's universal offer of advancement. He modeled that advancement, and he urged others along a comparable climb. The nation's progress opened prospects for all men. They had only to join in the march. Lincoln's bridge across the class divide was his own life. He had no need to contrive a special appeal to the poor because he gave everyone in his audience equal standing. Although Lincoln's orientation was not uniquely his, it placed him among a minority who stretched democracy's egalitarianism about as far as it would go to encompass America's male population.

MALE, not female. Lincoln's democracy was a fraternity, rooted in the man's world of law and politics and then extended nationwide. To a considerable degree Lincoln inherited these gender-laden conditions. Law and politics had long been male monopolies to which the new democracy now added a greater self-consciousness about spheres for men and women and a greater emphasis on personal connections within each sphere. Political life in Lincoln's time broke down into clusters of men who were bound together by mutual trust. A circle of this sort identified a politician's "friends"; other circles—some inside, some outside the politician's party—were his "enemies." Although these terms already had a history in Anglo-American politics, their very different usage in the late eighteenth century revealed a good deal about the changing values of partisanship in the early nineteenth. America's revolutionary leaders had employed friends and enemies to separate what they regarded as fundamental camps: the friends and enemies of liberty, for example, or of government. Now these terms referred to very personal support and hostility, to particular groupings of men who would determine a politician's rise or fall. Though political principles certainly mattered, circles of mutual trust established the actual ligaments of political organization, especially in anything relating to nominations and elections. The man who allowed principle to override loyalty in a vote to fill an office might ruin a lifetime's political reputation.

Along with these canons of comradeship and loyalty came a new expressiveness. Where the standard for gentlemen in the eighteenth century had been a cool self-control, the norms for respectable men in the early nineteenth greatly expanded the acceptable range of emotions, as the breathless, live-or-die language of the new democratic politics illustrated. Of course politics always carried an emotional charge for those whom it engaged deeply, and where that charge existed, some expression of it inevitably followed. Both before and after the arrival of democratic politics, however, those expressions occurred eruptively as moments of release in an otherwise bottled activity. The impact from such sudden floods of feeling might last a man's lifetime—Thomas Jefferson's memory of his response to Patrick Henry's oratory, for example, or Josephus Daniels's to the Cross of Gold speech in 1896. Between the 1820s and the 1850s, the enthusiasms, the sweeps from hope to despair, the sharp sensitivities toward friends and enemies, ran so normally through American politics that from a later perspective they gave the entire process a wild, volatile appearance. Apocalyptic pronouncements about the imminent collapse of a major party or the diabolical corruption of a government administration became ordinary parts of political discourse. Yet it was not that these Americans cared more deeply than other generations or that they suffered from a peculiar disease called antiparty politics. On the contrary, they made natural complements of party politics and emotional openness.

Hence in the basic units of political comradeship and loyalty, the fraternities, a language of affection interwove as a matter of course with other partisan business. "Jealousy," "pain," and "love" dotted the correspondence of political activists just as "tariff," "bank," and "railroad" did. "I loved him with the love that Jonathan had for David," General Urban Linder recalled of Stephen A. Douglas "—'A love that passeth the love of woman.' "[14] George Booker, seeking to strengthen his ties with a Virginia associate, Robert M. T. Hunter, reported the petulant complaint of a third fraternity member, Thomas H. Bayly: "When and how come you so fond of Hunter. You always loved Hunter better than you love me." Hunter, like other politicians who were growing more prominent, felt obliged to assure the multiplying members of his network "that I have not neglected you," for a sense of personal indifference could snap the ties of trust.[15] Associates were not slow in expressing their hurt feelings, as Archibald Yell of Arkansas demonstrated in a letter of remonstrance to his former Tennessee colleague James K. Polk: "I will not complain that I have not herd from you this winter. There is no crime . . . for me to bring in Judgement against you. I am ready to attribt. it to other causes rather than intentional neglect."[16] The bondings in politics were so commonplace that only the tightest warranted notice—the one, for example, between the "Siamese twins" of Washington, bachelor senators James Buchanan of

Pennsylvania and William R. D. King of Alabama, who were more maliciously known as he and she.

Comrades accentuated the maleness of political life by using it as a legitimizing cover for the disreputable behavior of respectable men. In effect, they capitalized on the seamy reputation that politics already had for its trafficking across the class line and proceeded to indulge in the drinking, swearing, and carousing that by the 1830s solid male citizens no longer had easily available to them—in fact, that an alliance of women and ministers was determined to deny them. Whatever ranked as a political victory also qualified as an occasion to hang one on in a gala, often very public celebration of it. "If you are beaten I fear we will find it hard to bear the rejoicing of your enemies here," one associate wrote Polk in 1835 during his bitter contest with a fellow Tennessean John Bell for Speaker of the House. Revealing more piety than foresight, he added: "Your friends will act prudently be the result what it may." Then again, maybe not. "After getting the news [of your victory]," another of Polk's colleagues reported to him a few days later, "a goodly number of the good and true Jackson boys . . . repaired to Vauxhall, where we screwed the necks off of a few dozen of champagne, under the roar of 48 rounds of cannon. After the 48 rounds and an immense deal of first rate enjoyment, the drum and fife arrived and soon collected several hundred men, who marched down town in regular order and after having passed round the square under constant discharges of muskets, the bells commenced ringing simultaneously at eleven o'clock [P.M.]. . . . Such shouting . . . I never heard; the good people of [Nashville] who were not in the secret, supposed the whole town was on fire. Every body was assured, some vexed to distraction . . . but it all passed off gloriously." From neighboring Mooresville came a briefer summary: "no lives lost and only a few wounded (not mortally) by the kicking of their pistols."[17]

Some politicians pursued these freedoms to the limit. Others tempered the raw male side of their politics with family commitments that distanced them from its loudest, bawdiest characteristics. Leaving home for a legislative session at the state capital, for example, might mark the peak of the reveling season. For Lincoln's fellow Whigs John J. Hardin and Orville Browning, on the other hand, a session of the legislature involved an extension of the well-mannered family socializing that they and their wives enjoyed at home. When Sarah Hardin did not accompany John to the capital, the devoted husband promptly reported to his "Dearest wife"—"I am very comfortably situated . . . & we have most excellent company"—with all the details about other wives and husbands among their mutual friends.[18] A common inclination toward respectable mixed company in the social side of politics turned the Hardins and Brownings into warm friends. In a similar vein, James Buchanan also preferred to combine his politics with a gossipy, heterosexual social life.

As a rule, men with strong ties to their families invested less of themselves in their fraternity lives. Hardin, immersed in an intergenerational network that spread between Kentucky and Illinois, illustrated this proposition. So did Polk, whose many connections with family relations revealed a closeness that his political friendships rarely matched. In politics, both men adopted a militia style of leadership, one that relied on mutual good will and personal trust but that put them a step apart from their associates. Appropriately, both did make political use of their militia connections, and fellow partisans addressed them as General Hardin and Colonel Polk. No one had to guess who presided over these fraternities. Stephen Douglas, a conscientious family man, developed a comparable pattern of political relations, felicitously termed "the Friar Tuck" style: the fraternity as a legion of good men and true who would always fight the good fight for Douglas and the Democracy. Bestowing special praise on those who had supported him first or stuck with him to the last, the Illinois senator chose dedication over intimacy to bind his circle of allies.

Lincoln fell far to the other end of the spectrum. Unlike Polk and Hardin, he more or less cut himself loose from the family web. As he escaped his childhood poverty, he turned his back on the family that embodied it, coolly insuring his parents against want but otherwise repudiating his father and offering routine acknowledgment to his step-mother. Although later in life he had brief enthusiasms for his genealogy, others prompted his interest, and it was never a lasting priority. Lincoln's dismissal of his childhood as "The short and simple annals of the poor" declared him radically, even brashly self-made by the standards of the mid-nineteenth century, for according to those lights the absence of a nurturing woman in Lincoln's account of his boyhood cast serious doubt on his strength of character. To vouch for the quality of his own rearing, Douglas inserted this stereotypical plea of mother to son in an autobiographical sketch of his departure from home: "My mother remonstrated, warned me of the dangers and temptations to which young men are exposed, and insisted upon my [finding] . . . a steady home and regular employment."[19] Lincoln walked off in silence, so the keepers of the Lincoln myth slipped the obligatory phrases into his mouth. Lincoln "spoke most kindly" of his mother and of his stepmother's "care of him," Leonard Swett imaginatively recalled. Henry Clay Whitney had Lincoln gush: "God bless my mother; all that I am or ever hope to be, I owe to her."[20]

Marriage did little to alter this picture of an almost perversely detached Lincoln. In contrast to John Hardin's urges to reunite with Sarah, Lincoln's urges took him away from his wife for long periods. Along with other men who gave their wives no place in their careers—Jefferson Davis, for example—Lincoln belittled and infantilized Mary Todd Lincoln in ways that practically denied them the possibility of a trusting, affectionate relationship. For his sons Lincoln felt very deep attachments, but these seemed quite separate from a general sense of family connectedness. They fitted as easily into the clutter of his law office as in the lap of domesticity.

Within the limits of a moody disposition, then, Lincoln was prepared to make full use of his fraternities. From his early years in politics he gravitated into groups: the "Long Nine" in the Illinois legislature; the "society, association, or what not" that he and other young politicians formed about 1837 in Springfield; the so-called Whig Junto.[21] His impulses inside these circles were egalitarian. As soon as he could, he slipped from under those people who cast him in an inferior position. In 1841 he severed the law partnership with his political sponsor John T. Stuart, and through his determined battle between 1843 and 1846 for the Whigs' congressional nomination he escaped a secondary role to either Edward D. Baker or John Hardin. Born in Hardin County, Kentucky, Lincoln had not climbed this far in order to live out his life in the Hardin district of Illinois.

Once freed from a superior, Lincoln showed little desire himself for a superior's privileges. Although he revealed no shyness in promoting causes, including himself, he rarely sought to direct as Hardin and Douglas did. Lincoln preferred to talk through issues rather than declare his positions on them. He liked to start early in a political undertaking and block out ample periods for reaching decisions because he needed time for personal exchange, persuasion, percolation. The same consensus style later characterized his dealings with executive officials. John Hay's report that as president Lincoln all but abandoned the efficient, impersonal routines of written correspondence suited these ingrained traits, as did the countless anecdotes from the war years about Lincoln's errant, idiosyncratic plunges into conversation with chance acquaintances. He always worked most comfortably through face-to-face relations, never through a chain of command.

To a considerable degree, Lincoln's ways here and elsewhere were simply the ways of the political fraternity. When he shed tears during a speech by Alexander Stephens in the House, for instance, Lincoln joined innumerable male contemporaries who recorded similar responses to their favorite orators. His language in attempting to revive his relationship with an Illinois associate had an equally familiar fraternal ring: "I am jealous because you did not write to me. Perhaps you have forgotten me."[22] True to the standards of personal trust that outranked all others in his world of politics, Lincoln, after an earnest, principled plea to a Democrat in behalf of the anti-Nebraska cause in 1854, ended with the axiom of the fraternity: "You may have given your word to vote for [the pro-Nebraska candidate] Major Harris, and if so, of course you will stick to it."[23]

Hints of a deeper emotional investment—and a greater emotional vulnerability—appeared now and then in Lincoln's reactions to what he interpreted as treason to the group. "To be wounded in the house of one's friends is perhaps the most grievous affliction that can befall a man," the reporter Noah Brooks had him say, rather pompously but nonetheless appropriately, in response to Republican abuse during his presidency.[24] A man as free from grudges as Lincoln still reserved a special bitterness for a few partisans who, he felt, had deceived or deserted him—the Judases of the fraternity. Of one fellow Whig he wrote passionately, "he *lied* in his *heart*." Of another he remembered above all that "in my greatest need of friends he was against me and for Baker." The man whom he had fought, Edward Baker, Lincoln not only forgave; he honored through the name of his second son. But nothing redeemed the deserter. In 1855, this man with so little meanness in him declared of the person who had tripped him in a run for the

United States Senate: "his defeat now gives me more pleasure than my own gives me pain."[25]

For a time early in the 1850s Lincoln's legal group dominated the fraternal side of his life. Always a significant part of the male comradeship he prized, Lincoln's legal circle served him most effectively as a fraternity while riding Illinois's Eighth Circuit. Here the mature Lincoln did tolerate a commander, for Judge David Davis clearly controlled the circuit fraternity. As the court and its retinue of lawyers and clients moved from town to town, Davis dispensed justice with an eye to his favorite lawyers during the day and cemented these relations each evening in the local tavern, where the court reconvened as a social club under the judge's broad-beamed aegis. "Ah! What glorious fun we had sometimes!" an insider recalled.[26] The more audacious members, particularly Ward Hill Lamon, Lincoln's wartime bodyguard, spread the horseplay of the evenings back into the daytime courts, where Davis allowed an occasional intrusion just as long as no one challenged his position as leader. It was Davis who kept the club's gate according to the nineteenth-century principles of egalitarianism: fully accept a man or completely reject him. "If Davis wanted [a newcomer in the group], he was warmly welcomed" and immediately drawn into the close circle of drinking and joking; but if Davis disliked him, "he was frozen out."[27]

Davis decided later that "Lincoln was happy as he could be on the circuit."[28] Others recalled that when colleagues broke the routine and went home, Lincoln stayed on the road longer than anyone else, following a schedule that kept him away from Springfield "over half the year."[29] Moreover, he stuck with the circuit riders well into the fifties when new district boundaries, railroad transportation, and the general level of Lincoln's practice seemed to eliminate the rationale for doing so. Choosing the male world of the circuit over family life, however, may have said nothing specific about his relations with Mary Todd Lincoln, for long ago he had acquired the reputation of a man who avoided women. "I never could get him in company with woman," his stepbrother John Hanks recalled of the teenage Lincoln; "he . . . [just] did not seek such company." The same word echoed from his Salem days: "everybody liked him . . . [but he] would just as lief the company were all men. . . ." Commenting on Lincoln in his twenties, only a woman could have reported matter-of-factly: "I knew Mr. L. well, he was a cold man, had no affection, was not social, was abstracted, thoughtful."[30] Men invariably remembered him as accessible, talkative, friendly.

The pattern did not significantly change with marriage. Lincoln shunned one after another of those social connections that might draw men and women together: "as little taste about dress and attire as anybody that ever was born"; "ate . . . without discrimination or choice"; "could not talk 'small talk.' "[31] In an age when women's sensibilities were considered incurably romantic, Lincoln seemed oblivious to them. At Niagara Falls he saw only a problem in physics. The report on Lincoln in his forties was the same as the one on Lincoln in his twenties—"Bashful and awkward in presence of ladies."[32] On circuit, a fellow member of the Davis club recalled, Lincoln would rather remain alone at a lodging house than join his comrades in an evening of mixed company. Here, meanwhile, was the man who enjoyed the endless exchanges in building a political consensus, who was everybody's favorite in the circuit fraternity, and who as president could take hold of a cabinet member and literally dance with joy. Although the married Lincoln kept a reserve from men as well as women, the emotions that did flow only moved comfortably through fraternity channels.

Lincoln's male associates justified these characteristics by contrasting the frivolities of the parlor with the serious stuff of law and politics. Lincoln concentrated on things that really mattered, they claimed. In fact, on an evening when Lincoln disdained the parlor, he was probably telling obscene stories. He was an incorrigible storyteller, everybody agreed, and reminiscences about his Springfield years identified these stories as "generally on the smutty order."[33] The salacious ones were "his funniest stories," reported his circuit companion Henry Clay Whitney.[34] Not only were these the hallmark of Lincoln's humor; that particular brand of humor helped to shape Lincoln's role in fraternity life. From their experience together in a Springfield political club, what one member could recollect about Lincoln thirty years later was the lewd verse he had contributed. At the evening gatherings on the circuit, Lincoln played "court jester," responding to the prods from Judge Davis to liven the company with another raunchy joke. In sum, Lincoln of Springfield had reason to be remembered as much for "an insane love of telling dirty and smutty stories" as for any other quality.[35]

To the regret of at least one comrade, Lincoln's repertoire of obscene stories disappeared with his fraternities. Because his taste seemed to run to the simple word play of the Joe Miller jokes, perhaps this fragment represented the genre. " 'Brown, why is a woman like a barrel?' . . . 'Well,' said Lincoln, 'you have to raise the hoops before you put the head in.' "[36] What mattered in the end was not the quality of the humor but the nature of its message. In a culture given to drawing lines, Lincoln etched one with particular force: men in and women out of his world of easy, warm relations. Of course Lincoln did not invent the misogynic style of the early nineteenth-century fraternities. It existed everywhere. Lewis Cass could bring general laughter from the Senate in 1855, for example, by interrupting a colleague's speech and blurting an irrelevant "Strong-minded women." Nevertheless, Lincoln made the demeaning of women his stock in trade—not a casual or occasional happening but the heart of his social style. To add as his friend Whitney did that he never told lewd stories in front of women merely underlined their fraternity-binding function. "If he was invited out to dine or to mingle in some social gathering," Herndon reported of Lincoln, ". . . at the very first opportunity he would have the men separated from their ladies and crowded close around him in one corner of the parlor, listening to one of his characteristic stories."[37]

In Lincoln's male circles, physical courage ranked among the most prized qualities of character, and bravery in an exalted cause perhaps highest of all. It was General Washington, not President Washington, who towered in the nation's pantheon, and it was the men who had but one life to give for their country who were immortalized in the heroic stories of the nineteenth-century schoolroom. Although Lincoln had difficulties with these martial standards, he never abandoned them. He was a slack militia captain, but he did join the militia. In 1842, when James Shields under Lincoln's and Mary Todd's goading challenged him to a duel, he behaved like the model of a reluctant participant. He chose weapons—"Cavalry broad swords of the largest size"—and conditions that would handcuff his little opponent and turn the event into a clang and clatter of futility.[38] Above all, he wanted the affair quietly settled, and he welcomed its peaceful solution with considerable relief. But what Lincoln did not do was simply to scotch the incident, as he might have done either with an immediate public apology or with a flat dismissal of the dueling code. Lincoln instructed his second in the affair to write that he "was wholly opposed to duelling, and would do anything to avoid it that might not degrade him in the estimation of himself and friends; but, if such degradation or a fight were the only alternatives, he would fight."[39] Courage measured the man, and each one had to meet its challenges as life presented them.

With this final piece from nineteenth-century culture in place, we can now see a rough solution to the puzzle of Lincoln's compassion. When rebels attacked his sacred union, they threatened an entire nation's progress, and in Lincoln's democratic scheme no cause could have been more genuinely popular than the defense of the United States: every last man had a vested interest in the American setting for his opportunities. Each of them, in fact, bore a double obligation to battle the enemy. As the president sent out seemingly endless waves of young men—including his own son Robert, he insisted—he could steel himself with the conviction that the nation's progress and the individual's manliness merged into a single commandment to fight and to suffer whatever was necessary in order to win.

Yet the same values of equality and fraternity—democratic inclusiveness and male exclusiveness—that stiffened Lincoln's wartime resolve also wrung his heart. The deadly march of the soldiers released the currents of his affection for men in an era that legitimized both the emotions and their expression. With none of the snobbishness and little of the prejudice that might have limited the range of these feelings, Lincoln swept the soldiers into a vast caravan of equals and wept for them all. When Lincoln thought of the poor and the floaters, he did not see cannon fodder. Each man of the lower class had the same rights to life's test as he did, and he never doubted that the best of them, too, could rise to the top of American society. In this great fraternity of equals, he and they belonged together. As the next generation of the fraternity bled, so did Lincoln. By his values he had to send them to slaughter; because of his affections he had to suffer for the terrible consequences. At the end of the nineteenth century a cohort of exceptional women, including Jane Addams, Florence Kelley, and Julia Lathrop, found in the compassionate Lincoln a singularly inspiring historical figure as they dedicated themselves to creating a more humane world for women and men alike.[40]

NOTES

1 / David Donald, *Lincoln's Herndon* (New York: Alfred A. Knopf, 1948), 93.

2 / E. B. Webb to Joseph Gillespie, August 8, 1844, Letters of Joseph Gillespie, Chicago Historical Society.

3 / Polk to Martin Van Buren, May 29, 1837, *Correspondence of James K. Polk,* ed. Herbert Weaver et al., 6 vols. to date (Nashville: Vanderbilt University Press, 1969–83), 4:131.

4 / Lincoln to Williamson Darley, October 3, 1845, *The Collected Works of Abraham Lincoln,* ed. Roy P. Basler, Marion Delores Pratt, and Lloyd A. Dunlap, 9 vols. (New Brunswick, N.J.: Rutgers University Press, 1953–55), 1:348.

5 / Jean H. Baker, *Affairs of Party: The Political Culture of Northern Democrats in the Mid-Nineteenth Century* (Ithaca: Cornell University Press, 1983), 123.

6 / *Collected Works of Lincoln,* 2:230.

7 / *Herndon's Life of Lincoln,* ed. Paul M. Angle (1889; reprint, New York: Albert and Charles Boni, 1936), 270–71, 210 (editor's note), 489.

8 / Jacob Greer to Polk, September 10, 1836, *Correspondence of Polk,* 3:726.

9 / Noah Brooks, *Washington in Lincoln's Time,* ed. Herbert Mitgang (1895; reprint, New York: Rinehart and Co., 1958), 219.

10 / *The Hidden Lincoln: From the Letters and Papers of William H. Herndon,* ed. Emanual Hertz (New York: Viking Press, 1938), 427.

11 / Gillespie to Herndon, December 8, 1866, ibid., 326.

12 / Forbes to Nassau William Senior, June 18, 1860, *Letters and Recollections of John Murray Forbes,* ed. Sarah Forbes Hughes, 2 vols. (Boston: Houghton Mifflin, 1900), 1:183.

13 / Eulogy to Henry Clay, July 6, 1852, *Collected Works of Lincoln,* 2:124.

14 / Usher F. Linder, *Reminiscences of the Early Bench and Bar of Illinois,* 2d ed. (Chicago: Chicago Legal News Co., 1879), 82. Here and elsewhere in this section of the essay I am especially indebted to the pioneering article by Carroll Smith-Rosenberg, "The Female World of Love and Ritual: Relations between Women in Nineteenth-Century America," *Signs* 1 (Autumn 1975): 1–29.

15 / Booker to Hunter, November 5, 1852, American Historical Association *Annual Report* (1916), vol. 2, *Correspondence of Robert M. T. Hunter 1826–1876,* ed. Charles Henry Ambler (Washington: Government Printing Office, 1918), 150.

16 / Yell to Polk, February 25, 1836, *Correspondence of Polk,* 3:516.

17 / Andrew C. Hays to Polk, December 12, 1835; A. O. P. Nicholson to Polk, December 20, 1835; Henry B. Kelsey to Polk, December 23, 1835, ibid., 395, 400, 409.

18 / John J. Hardin to Sarah E. Hardin, December 6, 1838, Hardin Family Papers, Chicago Historical Society.

19 / September 1, 1838, *The Letters of Stephen A. Douglas,* ed. Robert W. Johannsen (Urbana: University of Illinois Press, 1961), 57.

20 / Swett, "Mr. Lincoln's Story of His Own Life," in *Reminiscences of Abraham Lincoln,* ed. Allen Thorndike Rice (New York: North American Review, 1888), 457; Whitney, *Life on the Circuit with Lincoln,* ed. Paul M. Angle (1892; reprint, Caldwell, Idaho: Caxton Printers, 1940), 507.

21 / James H. Matheney's Statement, in Hertz, *Hidden Lincoln,* 371.

22 / Lincoln to Josephus Hewett, February 13, 1848, *Collected Works of Lincoln,* 1:450. Gordon Wood improved my understanding of this quotation.

23 / Lincoln to John M. Palmer, September 7, 1854, ibid., 2:228.

24 / Brooks, *Washington in Lincoln's Time*, 156.

25 / Fragment of a Letter [1849], Lincoln to Herndon, January 5, 1849; Lincoln to Elihu Washburne, February 9, 1855, *Collected Works of Lincoln*, 2:17, 19, 306.

26 / Linder, *Reminiscences of the Bench*, 183.

27 / Whitney, *Life on the Circuit*, 66.

28 / Hertz, *Hidden Lincoln*, 426–27.

29 / Angle, *Herndon's Life*, 249.

30 / John Hanks's Statement; N. W. Brandon to Herndon, August 3, 1865; Mrs. N. W. Edwards's Statement, in Hertz, *Hidden Lincoln*, 347, 284, 373.

31 / Whitney, *Life on the Circuit*, 55, 123, 470.

32 / Ibid., 59.

33 / Linder, *Reminiscences of the Bench*, 38.

34 / Whitney, *Life on the Circuit*, 66.

35 / Honorable H. E. Dummer's Statement, in Hertz, *Hidden Lincoln*, 385.

36 / C. C. Brown's Statement, ibid., 380. A bit of early eighteenth-century London doggerel suggests how time worn the joke already was in Lincoln's day:

> Then sometimes he stoops
> To take up the Hoops
> Of your Daughters as well as your Barrels.

Quoted in Paul S. Boyer, "Borrowed Rhetoric: The Massachusetts Excise Controversy of 1754," *William and Mary Quarterly* 21 (1964): 342.

37 / Angle, *Herndon's Life*, 343.

38 / Memorandum of Duel Instructions to Elias H. Merryman [September 19, 1842], *Collected Works of Lincoln*, 1:301.

39 / E. H. Merryman to Editors of the [Springfield] *Journal*, October 8, 1842, in Angle, *Herndon's Life*, 196.

40 / I am indebted to Rebecca Sherrick for information about the attitudes of Addams, Kelley, and Lathrop toward Lincoln.

DON E. FEHRENBACHER

★

The Words of Lincoln

" 'TIS A KIND OF GOOD DEED TO SAY WELL; AND YET WORDS
are no deeds." So declares Shakespeare's Henry VIII to Cardinal
Wolsey. The same distinction is made in several old adages. "Deeds are
fruits, words are but leaves," says one. "Words are but the shadows of
actions," says another. And according to still another: "A man of
words and not of deeds, is like a garden full of weeds." Yet the difference between word and deed has become increasingly blurred in the
modern age when so many combinations of words (such as "you're
fired") constitute acts, and so many physical acts (such as certain kinds
of terrorism) are essentially statements. Among modern public leaders
especially, important action is nearly always verbal. In the words of
a Jefferson, a Napoleon, or a Churchill one finds not only the record but
the substance of his principal deeds, as well as the clearest traces of his
character.

To study Abraham Lincoln, then, we must examine his words, and
not only the words that he wrote but also those that he uttered, in so far
as they are known. There, of course, one encounters difficulty, for
spoken words in the days before the phonograph were literally breaths
instantly dissolved in the air. Though sometimes captured by note-
taking when the occasion called for it, they were more often recon-
stituted through memory—memory exercised over lengths of time
varying from a few hours to half a century. Historical sources of this

kind have a curiously mixed status; they are not regarded as canonical but are nevertheless used extensively by biographers. More specifically, utterances of Lincoln not written out in his own hand or recorded in contemporary newspaper reports are generally excluded from the *Collected Works*.[1] Yet much of our impression of the man's character and style is based upon spoken words attributed to him in diaries, contemporary letters, and reminiscent writings.

Take, for instance, the countless putative examples of Lincoln's wit and humor that have appeared in print. They derive almost entirely from oral tradition and are therefore almost entirely uncanonical. Paul M. Zall, in his book *Abe Lincoln Laughing,* presents 325 items carefully selected from a much larger mass of material, including representative apocrypha, together with the stories that Lincoln "most likely told."[2] Of the 325, only 16 (about 5 percent) appear also in the *Collected Works,* and only 3 (less than 1 percent) exist in Lincoln's own handwriting.

But let us pursue this subject into the mainstream of Lincoln literature as represented by Stephen B. Oates's prime biography, *With Malice Toward None.* Choosing at random the Oates chapter on the five-month period between the election of 1860 and the firing on Fort Sumter, I counted some forty Lincoln quotations, ranging in length from several words to a dozen lines.[3] Three-quarters of them are spoken words, either taken down at the time or recollected later. Fewer than half of the forty items are drawn from the *Collected Works.* They include a series of excerpts from letters written to various Republican leaders enjoining them to resist compromise, and also a long string of quotations from the speeches Lincoln made on his journey to Washington.

The chapter is titled "My Troubles Have Just Begun," and it opens with the following sentence: " 'Well, boys,' he told newsmen the day after his election, 'your troubles are over now, mine have just begun.' " Oates cites as his source Charles M. Segal's book *Conversations with Lincoln,* where the quotation reads: "Well, boys, your troubles are over now, *but* mine have just begun."[4] Segal, in turn, cites an article by Samuel R. Weed, a St. Louis newspaperman. Written in 1882 ("apparently," Segal tells us, "from detailed notes made at the time"), the article remained unpublished until the *New York Times* printed it in 1932. The *Times* version of the quotation runs: "Well, boys, your

troubles are over now, but mine have just *commenced*." Nothing whatever is said about the article's having been based upon notes taken in
1860, and we are left wondering where Segal got the notion that it was.[5]
The purpose here is not to demonstrate that Oates should have titled his
chapter "My Troubles Have Just Commenced." It is rather to suggest
that if both Oates and Segal could modify a twelve-word quotation in
the process of copying it from text, we may with good reason suspect
much greater slippage between what Lincoln allegedly said in 1860 and
what Weed allegedly remembered in 1882. Even if one assumes the
honesty of this unknown man and overlooks the lack of corroborating
evidence that he ever spent any time in Lincoln's company, there remains the problem of what Daniel Aaron calls "the treachery of recollection."[6] The Weed article is, in short, dubious source material,
especially as a source of direct quotation.

Oates's chapter contains several other direct quotations of Lincoln
taken from recollective writings,[7] including one about a curious mysti-
cal experience. Some weeks after his election to the presidency, Oates
tells us, Lincoln lay down to rest on a sofa in his chamber.

> He glanced across the room at a looking glass on the bureau and
> saw himself reflected at almost full length. But his face had two
> separate and distinct images. Startled, he got up and approached
> the glass, but the illusion vanished. He lay back down, and the
> double image reappeared, clearer than before. Now one face was
> flushed with life, the other deathly pale. A chill passed through
> him. Later he told Mary about it and she became very upset. She
> interpreted the vision to mean that he would live through his first
> administration, but would die in his second. Lincoln tried to put it
> out of his mind, but "the thing would come up once in a while and
> give me a little pang, as though something uncomfortable had
> happened."[8]

Oates cites two authorities for this passage, *Washington in Lincoln's Time*
by Noah Brooks (1895) and the *Recollections of Abraham Lincoln* by Ward
Hill Lamon (1911). It is the Brooks memoir upon which Oates princi-
pally relies and from which he extracts the direct quotation attributed to
Lincoln. Brooks, in fact, published much the same account in *Harper's
Monthly* for July 1865, just eight months or so after the incident had
been related to him, he said, by Lincoln. Lamon's contribution lends

support to the Brooks version while differing from it in certain details, but the independence of his testimony is open to question. However, the main features of the story are also corroborated by the artist Francis Carpenter in his book *Six Months in the White House,* published in 1866. Carpenter mentions the recent Brooks article in a footnote and states that he did not read it until after his own account was written. That, if true, makes them independent witnesses to Lincoln's narration of the incident. Taking them all together, the effect of the Brooks, Lamon, and Carpenter recollections is partly corroboration and partly contradiction.[9]

According to Brooks, Lincoln talked about the double-image incident at the time of his reelection in 1864, saying that it had occurred at the time of his election in 1860. According to Carpenter, Lincoln talked about the incident at the time of his renomination in 1864, saying that it had occurred at the time of his nomination in 1860. According to Lamon, who splits the difference between the other two, Lincoln spoke of the incident at the time of his renomination in 1864, saying that it had occurred at the time of his election in 1860. It is Brooks alone who credits Mrs. Lincoln with the prophetic interpretation of the experience as signifying that her husband would not survive his second presidential term. Lamon asserts that Lincoln himself conceived the idea. Carpenter declares that Lincoln, in telling him the story, attached no such gloomy significance to it. As for the quotation that Oates draws from the Brooks memoir ("the thing would come up once in a while and give me a little pang, as though something uncomfortable had happened"),[10] it is more or less contradicted by Carpenter, who quotes Lincoln as saying that the phenomenon ceased to trouble him after he decided that it was the result of some natural principle of refraction or optics. Furthermore, the passage in question is part of a 300-word paragraph that Brooks ventured to enclose in quotation marks, while claiming only that he was giving Lincoln's "own words, as nearly as they could then be recalled" eight months after he had heard them. Thus the phrasing of the quotation is probably a Lincoln-Brooks mixture at best.

It would be difficult to find a better illustration of how recollective writings can be at once valuable and dubious as primary historical sources. Here, the direct quotation in question is suspect; the dates are confused; Lincoln's feelings about his curious illusion are in doubt; and Mary Lincoln's spooky prescience is not easy to swallow. Nevertheless, we are left with strong evidence that Lincoln did see the double image in 1860, that the incident made a considerable impression on his mind, that he spoke of it more than once in 1864, and that at least some part of the substance of his account can be summarized with some confidence. This information, though not given the canonical seal of inclusion in the *Collected Works,* is nevertheless an item likely to be useful in the study of Lincoln's intellectual and emotional life.

Further on in the chapter, Oates describes a meeting on April 4, 1861, between Lincoln and John B. Baldwin, a Virginia Unionist. Lincoln wanted the Virginia state convention, then sitting, to adjourn. "But Baldwin," Oates tells us, "insisted that Lincoln must pull out of Sumter first, warning that if he didn't and if a shot were fired, then . . . Virginia would secede in forty-eight hours." Lincoln remained firm, however. " 'Sir,' he said of Baldwin's demand, 'that is impossible.' "[11] Oates's authority for this account is the record of Baldwin's testimony before the Joint Committee on Reconstruction in 1866.[12] But when one reads the entire passage, it becomes apparent that Lincoln's alleged response—"Sir, that is impossible"—was allegedly addressed, not to the demand for evacuation of Fort Sumter, as Oates asserts, but rather to Baldwin's warning that otherwise Virginia would secede. In other words, Baldwin in 1866 was portraying the Lincoln of 1861 as a man who stubbornly and obtusely refused to believe that hostilities at Sumter would drive Virginia out of the Union. Furthermore, as a historical source, this testimony has all the weaknesses of other recollective material, and it also inspires doubt because it was so patently self-serving.

There are also quotations in the Oates chapter drawn from the diary of Orville H. Browning, from a contemporary memorandum of John G. Nicolay, and from a contemporary political letter to Simon Cameron.[13] This kind of recollective material inspires considerable confidence because such a short time elapsed between the event and the recording of it. Of course the value of such evidence still depends upon the competence, objectivity, and plain honesty of the witness. And sometimes there can be confusion about whose words, precisely, are being reproduced. For example, Oates quotes Lincoln as saying to Browning in February 1861 that only "the surrender of everything worth preserving" would satisfy the South. But what Browning recorded in his diary was this: "He agreed with me no concession by the free States short of a surrender of every thing worth preserving, and contending for would satisfy the South." Thus the words and the thought actually came from Browning, and Lincoln merely acquiesced in them.[14]

Likewise relatively credible are those quotations in the chapter that come from contemporary newspaper articles written by reporters after talking with Lincoln.[15] The lapse of time between hearing and recording was brief, and in each instance there is the possibility that notes were taken on the spot. Indeed, contemporary newspaper sources have been considered reliable enough for inclusion in the *Collected Works,* although such inclusion has generally been limited to reports of public speeches.

Oates was on the solidest ground, of course, in the numerous quotations he drew from the *Collected Works.* Yet even within those canonical covers there are different levels of credibility—newspaper summaries of speeches, for instance, do not have the same status as autograph letters signed. Although the ten volumes of the *Collected Works* constitute a splendid editorial achievement, they do contain a few questionable patches. One conspicuous example is the letter that Lincoln supposedly wrote to General James S. Wadsworth early in 1864. This document has come to be regarded as at least partly spurious, for its provenance is unsatisfactory, and it does not ring true with respect to Lincoln's attitude toward racial equality at that date.[16] In contrast, there is a much fainter breath of doubt associated with the famous letter of condolence to Mrs. Lydia Bixby. Since the original letter was lost, and its words survived only as they were printed in a Boston newspaper, there is no way of verifying or disproving some dubious gossip that attributes the authorship to John Hay. Nevertheless, there seems to be general agreement among scholars in the field that the words of the Bixby letter are characteristically and peculiarly Lincoln's.[17]

For one other interesting example of a questionable patch in the *Collected Works,* let us examine a portion of Lincoln's famous House Divided speech:

[1]   Either the *opponents* of slavery, will arrest the further spread of it, and place it where the public mind shall rest in the belief that it is in course of ultimate extinction; or its *advocates* will

push it forward, till it shall become alike lawful in *all* the States, *old* as well as *new*—*North* as well as *South*.

[2]   Have we no *tendency* to the latter condition?

[3]   Let any one who doubts, carefully contemplate that now almost complete legal combination—piece of *machinery* so to speak—compounded of the Nebraska doctrine, and the Dred Scott decision. Let him consider not only *what work* the machinery is adapted to do, and *how well* adapted; but also, let him study the *history* of its construction, and trace, if he can, or rather *fail,* if he can, to trace the evidences of design, and concert of action, among its chief bosses, from the beginning.

[4]   But, so far, *Congress* only, had acted; and an *indorsement* by the people, *real* or apparent, was indispensable, to *save* the point already gained, and give chance for more.

[5]   The new year of 1854 found slavery excluded from more than half the States by State Constitutions, and from most of the national territory by Congressional prohibition.

[6]   Four days later, commenced the struggle, which ended in repeating that Congressional prohibition.

[7]   This opened all the national territory to slavery; and was the first point gained.

[8]   This necessity had not been overlooked; but had been provided for, as well as might be, in the notable argument of "*squatter sovereignty,*". . .[18]

There is something wrong in the above passage, and I confess that it had to be pointed out to me by a Lincoln scholar with a keener eye than mine—namely, George B. Forgie. Paragraph 4 is plainly a non sequitur, and so is paragraph 8. But those lapses of logic disappear and everything is made right if one simply picks up paragraph 4 and inserts it between paragraph 7 and paragraph 8.

The error of transposition is incorporated in three books of selected Lincoln writings that were derived from the *Collected Works*—one edited by the late T. Harry Williams (1957), one by me (1964), and one by Richard N. Current (1967).[19] The error also appears in Paul M. Angle's edition of the Lincoln-Douglas debates titled *Created Equal?* (1958).[20] Yet Robert W. Johannsen's edition of the debates (1965) has the text in the right order, and so does the Nicolay and Hay *Complete Works* (1894).[21] In the last two works, moreover, the paragraphs are generally longer, and the profuse italicization of the *Collected Works* is missing.

There are, in fact, two original sources of the House Divided address. Roy P. Basler and the other editors of the *Collected Works* used the version published in the *Illinois State Journal* on June 18, 1858, two days after Lincoln's delivery of the speech; so did Paul M. Angle. This text was presumably set from Lincoln's own manuscript copy. If we can believe the recollective testimony of journalist Horace M. White, both he and Lincoln read proof of the speech in the *Journal* office.[22] Yet, if so, neither discovered the transposition of paragraphs. That the error was not present in the manuscript becomes clear when we examine the other original source—namely, a "phonographic"—that is, a stenographic—report of the speech, taken down as the words fell from Lincoln's lips, and printed in the *Chicago Tribune* on June 19. There, the sentences are in their logical order, italics are absent, and the paragraphing is different, having been arbitrarily determined by the stenographer. It was the *Tribune* version that Lincoln put into his scrapbook and later provided for inclusion with the Lincoln-Douglas debates when they were published as a book in 1860.[23] That was the text followed by Nicolay and Hay in the 1890s, by Arthur Brooks Lapsley in his 1905 edition of Lincoln's writings,[24] and by Robert Johannsen in the 1960s.

Thus, two somewhat different versions of the House Divided speech have been perpetuated, emanating from different sources, and proceeding down through the years like two columns of soldiers marching along separate but parallel roads. One source is a slightly garbled copy of the words Lincoln *wrote*. The other is a stenographic record, no doubt less than perfect, of the words he *spoke*. Clearly, the best version would be one making intelligent use of both sources. I can find only one scholar who employed such strategy, and that, ironically, was Roy P. Basler—not in the *Collected Works,* but in an earlier book, *Abraham Lincoln: His Speeches and Writings.* There, Basler followed the text of the *Illinois State Journal,* with "a few emendations" taken from the *Chicago*

Tribune version. His most important change was to correct the error of the transposed paragraphs—a correction that he failed to make as chief editor of the *Collected Works*.[25]

Errors in the *Collected Works* are so few and far between that a biographer who quoted Lincoln only from its pages would have secure footing indeed, but his work would be impoverished as a consequence. He could not, for example, repeat Lincoln's comparison of Horace Greeley to an old shoe, "so rotten that nothing can be done with him"; or his comparison of Salmon P. Chase to a bluebottle fly, laying eggs in "every rotten spot" it could find; or his comparison of a dwindling army on the march to a "shovelful of fleas pitched from one place to another."[26] And a biographer so fastidious would likewise have to omit such gems as Lincoln's reported comment in pardoning a certain condemned soldier: "If a man had more than one life, I think a little hanging would not hurt this one"; and his response to a pestering favor seeker, as remembered by John Hay: "Now, my man, go away! I cannot attend to all these details. I could as easily bail out the Potomac with a spoon."[27] The *Collected Works*, after all, comprises not only the *writings* of Lincoln but also many of his utterances as recorded by newspaper reporters. Outside the *Collected Works*, in addition, there is a great accumulation of spoken words attributed to Lincoln that cannot be ignored. Yet, as examination of a single chapter in one major Lincoln study has demonstrated, to use this rich resource is to walk on treacherous ground.

What we need, and may never have, is a systematic, critically evaluative compilation of all the utterances, whether quoted or merely summarized, that have been attributed to Lincoln in contemporary and recollective primary sources. Until some such authoritative treasury of his spoken words is provided, several cautionary rules respecting the use of such material may be in order.

First, it should be recognized that many a quotation has a provenance too weak and/or a substance too dubious to be incorporated in serious historical writing.

Second, much recollected utterance, and especially the lengthy remark recalled over a long span of time, should probably be treated as, at best, *indirect* rather than *direct* quotation.

Third, insofar as the pace of the narrative or argument will allow it, the reader should be given some measure of a quotation's authenticity.

Fourth and finally, the interpretative weight placed upon a quotation should be compatible with the quality of its authentication.

Maximum accuracy in quoting Lincoln is not merely a pedantic ideal. It becomes increasingly a necessity as ever more ponderous burdens of discovered meaning are laid upon his words by psychoanalytic scholars and other deep readers of historical texts. Charles B. Strozier, in his psychohistorical study of Lincoln, builds an elaborate structure of Freudian diagnosis upon two sentences that Lincoln wrote about shooting a wild turkey.[28] Whatever one may think of his interpretation, it rests on the unimpeachable foundation of a handwritten Lincoln document.[29] Elsewhere in the book, while analyzing Lincoln's periodic bouts of depression, Strozier makes the flat assertion that "political defeat could devastate Lincoln." But the proof he offers consists almost entirely of the following statement:

> There is some evidence that in 1858 Lincoln was distraught at the loss to Douglas. On the evening of the defeat he said to his friend Henry C. Whitney that his life had been "an abject and lamentable failure." Whitney reported: "I never saw any man so radically and thoroughly depressed, so completely steeped in the bitter waters of hopeless despair."[30]

Here is what Whitney actually wrote, however:

> On January 5th, the day of Douglas' last election to the U.S. Senate by the legislature—I was alone with Mr. Lincoln from 2 o'clock P.M. till bed-time—and I feel authorized to say that no man in the state was so gloomy, dejected and dispirited, and no man so surely and heartily deemed his life to have been an abject and lamentable failure, as he then considered his to have been. I never saw any man so radically and thoroughly depressed, so completely steeped in the bitter waters of hopeless despair.[31]

Plainly, Whitney does not assert that Lincoln called his life "an abject and lamentable failure." The words and the thought are Whitney's, not Lincoln's. They are part of a description of Lincoln's mood on a particular day in 1859, as Whitney supposedly remembered it more than thirty years later. Moreover, Whitney's reputation for honest recollection is a tainted one, and, as Strozier acknowledges in a footnote, there is countervailing testimony that Lincoln took the senatorial defeat in stride.[32] Whitney's account is therefore a very weak peg upon which to hang a significant conclusion about Lincoln's temperament.

To illustrate minutely the importance that precise quotation can assume, let me return to the House Divided speech and one of its most famous sentences: "I believe this government cannot endure, permanently half *slave* and half *free.*" In the *Illinois State Journal*'s version (and therefore in the *Collected Works*), there is a comma after the word "endure," presumably put there deliberately by Lincoln. In the *Chicago Tribune*'s version and others derived from it, that comma is omitted. The omission has the effect of linking "endure" with "permanently," thereby causing Lincoln to say little more than that the nation cannot go on forever divided between freedom and slavery—a rather weak prediction of crisis at some future time. But with the comma inserted, "permanently" is separated from "endure" and associated with the second half of the sentence. The shade of meaning changes as a consequence. The Union, Lincoln is saying, cannot survive as a nation permanently divided into free and slave sections. And since each section is already committed to the permanency of its condition with respect to slavery, this means that the crisis is already at hand. Thus the comma tends to radicalize the sentence. Was that Lincoln's intention? Or was the comma, instead, nothing more than eccentric punctuation—or perhaps just an error introduced by the printer? Whenever he quoted the sentence in later correspondence, Lincoln omitted the comma, and he repeatedly explained the House Divided passage in moderate tones. But these facts are not conclusive; for, as the paragraphing makes clear, he was quoting from the commaless *Chicago Tribune* version, which he had put into his scrapbook; and as a presidential candidate he needed to dissociate himself from the radical implications of the speech.[33]

Testing the historical value of attributed spoken words is a more complex and inconclusive enterprise than testing the value of written words. With documents, the problem of authenticity is largely a physical matter (paper, ink, handwriting) that can be dealt with separately from the problem of the credibility of testimony; whereas with attributed words, the problem of authenticity is itself largely a matter of credibility. For example, if A writes to B saying, "C tried to bribe me yesterday," the authenticity of the quotation depends upon the genuineness of the letter as an artifact, while its credibility as historical evidence depends upon A's reliability as a witness, considering the circumstances in which he wrote. But if A writes in a memoir, "Just before the election, B telephoned and said, 'C has just tried to bribe me,' " the authenticity of the quotation depends upon A's reliability as a recollective witness of the utterance, while its credibility depends upon B's reliability as a witness of the event. Reliability will vary, not only from person to person but also from situation to situation. For instance, one finds it relatively easy to believe Herndon when he tells us that Lincoln said to him in 1861, "Give our clients to understand that the election of a President makes no change in the firm of Lincoln and Herndon." But I for one become more suspicious when he recalls telling his partner in 1858, after hearing a preview reading of the House Divided address, "Lincoln, deliver that speech as read and it will make you President."[34]

There is no simple formula for judging the authenticity of recollected utterances. One looks first for independent corroboration but rarely finds it. The elapse of time between the utterance and the recording of it is always significant, though never conclusive. Certainly the kind of record in which the quotation appears, as well as the relationship of the quoter to the person quoted, must be carefully weighed. But every recollection of spoken words is a separate problem in historical method.[35] In each instance, the historian must call upon his professional experience, his knowledge of the particular historical context, and his common sense to make a judgment of probability—not only about the authenticity of the quotation, but also about how close it comes to being a verbatim report as distinguished from a mere paraphrase.

Of course, the historian studies words in a search for meanings. To know as fully and accurately as possible what Lincoln really said is the firmest foundation upon which to build an understanding of what he and his life meant. But accurate quotation of a person's words is only a beginning. It does not ensure their satisfactory interpretation.

Consider, for instance, the exclamatory comment that Lincoln jotted down sometime during or soon after his debates with Douglas: "Negro equality! Fudge!! How long, in the government of a God, great enough to make and maintain this Universe, shall there continue knaves to vend, and fools to gulp, so low a piece of demagougeism as this."[36] LaWanda Cox, in her book *Lincoln and Black Freedom,* says that this passage "can be read as scorn for his opponent's appeal to prejudice, and scorn for those who applauded that appeal."[37] But such a reading misjudges the direction of Lincoln's anger. "Fudge," after all, means "nonsense," and Lincoln was talking, not about the repulsiveness of racial prejudice, but rather about the absurdity and dishonesty of the charge that he, and Republicans generally, favored racial equality. Denying the charge again and again during the senatorial campaign, he bitterly resented the "demagougeism" that forced him to do so.

Consider also the meaning that has been read into those paragraphs of the young Lincoln's Lyceum speech in which he discussed the possible emergence of an American usurper driven by a hunger for renown. "Is it unreasonable . . . to expect," he asked, "that some man possessed of the loftiest genius, coupled with ambition sufficient to push it to its utmost stretch, will at some time, spring up among us?"[38] Edmund Wilson seems to have been the first writer to suggest that in this passage Lincoln projected himself into the demonic role he was so eloquently describing. Subsequently, there have been several elaborations of the same theme, the effect of which is to make the nation's tragic destiny in the mid-nineteenth century a mere extension of Lincoln's towering ambition and relentless will.[39]

It is no doubt true that anyone seeking to explain the feelings of a historical figure must establish a bond of empathy, however synthetic and temporary the bond may be. But aside from such normal literary identification with one's subject of the moment, the lifetime record of Lincoln's words and behavior lends little support to Wilson's conjecture and the line of interpretation associated with it. On the contrary, much of that record points in the opposite direction. Perhaps the greatest weakness of the interpretation is that it endows Lincoln with far more control over the course of events and over his own fate than common sense will accept or the facts warrant. But in addition, it ignores two models that Lincoln very likely had in mind. One was the colossal figure of Napoleon Bonaparte, dead only seventeen years at the time of the Lyceum speech. The other, even closer at hand, was Andrew Jackson, whom Whigs had so recently been calling a violator of the Constitution and a would-be tyrant.[40]

Sound interpretation of any historical text begins with an effort to determine the author's intended meaning. That includes paying attention to context and circumstance, keeping a sharp eye out for irony and other kinds of indirection, discriminating between denotative and connotative meanings, and coming to terms with the fact that intentions may be overt, or deliberately concealed, or at work only beneath the surface of consciousness.

The complexity that sometimes encumbers a search for intent can be illustrated with Lincoln's famous letter to Horace Greeley, in which he declared: "My paramount object in this struggle *is* to save the Union, and is *not* either to save or destroy slavery. If I could save the Union without freeing *any* slave I would do it, and if I could save it by freeing *all* the slaves I would do it; and if I could save it by freeing some and leaving others alone I would also do that."[41] By itself, this pronouncement bears some resemblance to Stephen A. Douglas's notorious assertion during the Lecompton controversy that he did not care whether slavery was "voted down or voted up" in Kansas.[42] But the letter will be misunderstood if it is read as a straightforward statement of Lincoln's political and ethical priorities, with the Union counting for everything and slavery for nothing. Lincoln's ostensible neutralism about slavery was misleading—and intentionally so. He had, in fact, already committed himself to emancipation, had drafted a proclamation, and was using the exchange with Greeley, as Benjamin P. Thomas says, "to prepare the people for what was coming."[43] Preservation of the Union and abolition of slavery were already bound together as twin purposes of the Civil War. Saving the Union had become more than an end in itself. It was also the indispensable means of achieving emancipation. But Lincoln, for reasons of political strategy, had to put it the other way around, viewing emancipation, first, as a *possible* means, and eventually, as a *necessary* means, of saving the Union. And still there is more to be said. To this perception of cool calculation and dissembled purpose in the Greeley letter one should add some understanding of the deeper uncertainties with which Lincoln contemplated the relation of the war to emancipation, and of emancipation to the future of the nation.

Along with the *intended* meaning of Lincoln's words, one must consider their *effective* meaning—that is, what they were *understood* to mean by his primary and his secondary audiences, and also what *consequences* they may have produced. There is a Thomas Nast cartoon that dramatizes how differently the North and South understood the first inaugural. It presents two Abraham Lincolns, one dressed as a prince of peace, the other armed as a god of war.[44] More difficult for the modern mind to comprehend is how the Emancipation Proclamation, perhaps the greatest document of social reform in American history, could have been understood, not only in the Confederacy but also by the *London Times,* as a barbarous effort to incite servile rebellion.[45] To seek the *consequential* meaning of words is to treat them as actions and thus pursue one's study into the realm of historical causation. Lincoln's famous interrogation of Douglas at Freeport is a good example of an utterance whose meaning has come to consist almost entirely in the consequences attributed to it. Likewise, his letters opposing compromise in the secession winter of 1860–61 have little meaning apart from the formidable question of whether they were enough to make the difference between reconciliation and disunion.

Besides their intended meanings and effective meanings within a definite historical context, some of Lincoln's words have acquired *transcendent* meaning as contributions to the permanent literary treasure of the nation. Just why his prose at its best is so splendid, so memorable, has been pondered by all sorts of critics. Edmund Wilson is one of those who emphasize the leanness and muscular strength of Lincoln's style, compared with the more ornate oratorical fashion of the day.[46] Yet, in his more formal pieces especially, Lincoln employed some of the structures and rhetorical devices of eighteenth-century expository writing. In the Gettysburg Address, for example, one scholar finds "two antitheses, five cases of anaphora, eight instances of balanced phrases and clauses, thirteen alliterations."[47] Several critics stress the richness and vigor of Lincoln's imagery, drawn as it was from everyday American experience and culture.[48] Jacques Barzun speaks of his gift of rhythm, "developed to a supreme degree," and of an extraordinary capacity for verbal discipline. "Lincoln," he says, "acquired his power by exacting obedience from words."[49]

Lincoln's literary skill is perhaps most open to view in those instances when he took someone else's prose and molded it to his own use. A prime example is the plea for reconciliation in the final paragraph of the first inaugural, a paragraph drafted originally by his secretary of state, William H. Seward. Let us look at just the short opening sentence. Seward wrote: "I close." Lincoln changed it to: "I am loth to close." The improvement in cadence is obvious enough, but also, the addition of three words makes the sentence throb with connotative meanings and emotive force. It expresses an almost elegiac reluctance to conclude his discussion of the crisis—a sense of remnant opportunities slipping away, of a cherished world about to be lost. In that vein Lincoln then proceeds with his moving but hopeless appeal to old "bonds of affection," to "mystic chords of memory," and to "the better angels of our nature."[50]

Here, then, was an occasion calling for eloquence; here was an ear keenly tuned to the music of the English language; here was intellectual grasp and moral urgency; here was great emotional power under firm artistic control. Here, in short, was the mastery that we associate with genius.

NOTES

1 / *The Collected Works of Abraham Lincoln,* ed. Roy P. Basler, Marion Delores Pratt, and Lloyd A. Dunlap, 9 vols. (New Brunswick, N.J.: Rutgers University Press, 1953–55), 1:ix.

2 / Paul M. Zall, *Abe Lincoln Laughing: Humorous Anecdotes from Original Sources by and about Abraham Lincoln* (Berkeley: University of California Press, 1982), 10. The most exhaustive study is Wayne Lee Garner, "Abraham Lincoln and the Uses of Humor" (Ph.D. diss., University of Iowa, 1963).

3 / Stephen B. Oates, *With Malice Toward None: The Life of Abraham Lincoln* (New York: Harper and Row, 1977), 195–227.

4 / Charles M. Segal, ed., *Conversations with Lincoln* (New York: G. P. Putnam's Sons, 1961), 38.

5 / *New York Times Magazine,* February 14, 1932, 8–9, 21.

6 / Daniel Aaron, "The Treachery of Recollection: The Inner and the Outer History," in *Essays on History and Literature,* ed. Robert H. Bremner ([Columbus]: Ohio State University Press, 1969), esp. 19, where he writes: "How true, really, are the tales from the horse's mouth? Eyewitness accounts of a murder or accident, we are told, often contradict each other. How much more untrustworthy may be the recollections of people who have conscious or unconscious motives for selective remembering or forgetting, who are themselves parties to the events described, whose view of the past is blurred by ignorance, hostility, or sentimentality? . . . written history concocted from such sources can become little more than hypotheses about what might have happened." Aaron is talking particularly about oral history, but his remarks are no less applicable to written reminiscence.

7 / Oates, *With Malice Toward None,* 196.

8 / Oates quotes from works by Donn Piatt (197), Thurlow Weed (200), William H. Herndon (201, 207), and Henry Villard (213–14).

9 / Noah Brooks, *Washington in Lincoln's Time,* ed. Herbert Mitgang (1895, reprint, New York: Rinehart and Co., 1958), 198–200; Brooks, "Personal Recollections of Abraham Lincoln," *Harper's New Monthly Magazine* 31 (July 1865): 224–25; Ward Hill Lamon, *Recollections of Abraham Lincoln, 1847–1865,* ed. Dorothy Lamon Taillard (Washington: published by the editor, 1911), 112–13; F. B. Carpenter, *Six Months in the White House*

with Abraham Lincoln: The Story of a Picture (New York: Hurd and Houghton, 1866), 163–65.

10 / In the quotation Oates departs slightly from his source, *Washington in Lincoln's Time,* which reads: "the thing would once in a while come up, and give me a little pang as if something uncomfortable had happened."

11 / Oates, *With Malice Toward None,* 224–25.

12 / Oates cites Segal, *Conversations with Lincoln,* 102–7. Segal's source was *Report of the Joint Committee on Reconstruction, House Reports,* 39th Cong., 1st sess. (Serial 1273), No. 30, part 2, 102–6. Under questioning, Baldwin acknowledged, "My literal memory is not good." But he insisted that his ability to recall the substance of what he had heard was "unusually good."

13 / Oates, *With Malice Toward None,* 201, 203, 207, 222. Oates cites the Browning diary and the Nicolay memorandum directly. The quotation from the letter to Cameron on 203 was taken from Reinhard H. Luthin, *The Real Abraham Lincoln* (Englewood Cliffs, N. J.: Prentice-Hall, 1960), 248.

14 / *The Diary of Orville Hickman Browning,* ed. Theodore Calvin Pease and James G. Randall, 2 vols. (Springfield: Illinois State Historical Library, 1925–33), 1:453.

15 / Oates, *With Malice Toward None,* 197, 198, with quotations from the *New York Tribune,* from Henry Villard's *Lincoln on the Eve* (a collection of dispatches to the *New York Herald*), and from the *Philadelphia Bulletin,* as copied in the *New York Times,* as reprinted in Segal, *Conversations with Lincoln.*

16 / *Collected Works of Lincoln* 7: 101–2; Ludwell H. Johnson, "Lincoln and Equal Rights: The Authenticity of the Wadsworth Letter," *Journal of Southern History* 32 (1966): 83–87.

17 / *Collected Works of Lincoln* 8: 116–17; Roy P. Basler, "Who Wrote the 'Letter to Mrs. Bixby'?" in his *A Touchstone for Greatness: Essays, Addresses, and Occasional Pieces about Abraham Lincoln* (Westport, Conn.: Greenwood Press, 1975), 110–19.

18 / *Collected Works of Lincoln* 2: 461–62.

19 / *Abraham Lincoln: Selected Speeches, Messages, and Letters,* ed. T. Harry Williams (New York: Rinehart and Co., 1957), 76; *Abraham Lincoln: A Documentary Portrait Through His Speeches and Writings,* ed. Don E. Fehrenbacher (New York: New American Library, 1964), 95–96; Richard N. Current, ed., *The Political Thought of Abraham Lincoln* (Indianapolis: Bobbs-Merrill Co., 1967), 95–96.

20 / *Created Equal?: The Complete Lincoln-Douglas Debates of 1858,* ed. Paul M. Angle (Chicago: University of Chicago Press, 1958), 2.

21 / Robert W. Johannsen, *The Lincoln-Douglas Debates of 1858* (New York: Oxford University Press, 1965), 14–15; John G. Nicolay and John Hay, *Abraham Lincoln, Complete Works: Comprising His Speeches, Letters, State Papers, and Miscellaneous Writings,* 2 vols. (New York: Century Co., 1894), 1:240–41.

22 / William H. Herndon and Jesse W. Weik, *Abraham Lincoln: The True Story of a Great Life,* 2 vols. (New York: D. Appleton and Co., 1892), 2:92. In this revised edition of their book, Herndon and Weik printed Horace White's recollection as follows: "I sat at a short distance from Mr. Lincoln when he delivered the 'house-divided-against-itself' speech, on the 17th [*sic*] of June. This was delivered from manuscript, and was the only one I ever heard him deliver in that way. When it was concluded he put the manuscript in my hands and asked me to go to the *State Journal* office and read the proof of it. I think it had already been set in type. Before I had finished this task Mr. Lincoln himself came into the composing room of the *State Journal* and looked over the revised proofs. He said to me

that he had taken a great deal of pains with this speech, and that he wanted it to go before the people just as he had prepared it."

23 / *Political Debates between Hon. Abraham Lincoln and Hon. Stephen A. Douglas, in the Celebrated Campaign of 1858, in Illinois* . . . (Columbus, Ohio: Follett, Foster and Co., 1860).

24 / Arthur Brooks Lapsley, *The Writings of Abraham Lincoln,* 8 vols. (New York: G. P. Putnam's Sons, 1905–1906), 3:2–3.

25 / Roy P. Basler, *Abraham Lincoln: His Speeches and Writings* (Cleveland: World Publishing Co., 1946), 372–81. The transposing was done by one of the assistant editors of the *Collected Works* in the process of collating the *Journal* and *Tribune* texts, but Basler, the chief editor, assumes ultimate responsibility for failing to catch the error. Basler to the author, May 9, 1985.

26 / Tyler Dennett, ed., *Lincoln and the Civil War in the Diaries and Letters of John Hay* (New York: Dodd, Mead and Co., 1939), 53, 110; Howard K. Beale, ed., *Diary of Gideon Welles, Secretary of the Navy Under Lincoln and Johnson,* 3 vols. (New York: W. W. Norton and Co., 1960), 2:112.

27 / John Hay, "Life in the White House in the Time of Lincoln," in *The Addresses of John Hay* (New York: Century Co., 1907), 324–25.

28 / Charles B. Strozier, *Lincoln's Quest for Union: Public and Private Meanings* (New York: Basic Books, Inc., 1982), 25–28.

29 / *Collected Works of Lincoln,* 4:62. For my critique of Strozier's wild turkey hypothesis, see "In Quest of the Historical Lincoln," *Reviews in American History* 11 (1983): 15–16.

30 / Strozier, *Lincoln's Quest for Union,* 209.

31 / Henry C. Whitney, *Life on the Circuit with Lincoln* (Boston: Estes and Lauriat, 1892), 27–28. Strozier cites a later edition, edited by Paul M. Angle (Caldwell, Idaho: Caxton Printers, 1940), 51.

32 / Strozier, *Lincoln's Quest for Union,* 259. Angle's introduction to the 1940 edition of *Life on the Circuit* provides information about Whitney's occasionally disreputable role in Lincoln scholarship. Whitney's assertion that he found Lincoln in his office at 2:00 P.M. on January 5, 1859, and spent the rest of the day alone with him is open to question because records indicate that Lincoln had at least three cases in court on that day.

33 / Basler, in *Abraham Lincoln: His Speeches and Writings,* 381, calls attention to the comma as an example of how the *State Journal* version of the speech reveals "the oral emphasis Lincoln gave to each sentence, phrase, and word."

34 / *Herndon's Life of Lincoln,* ed. Paul M. Angle (1889; reprint, Cleveland: World Publishing Co., 1949), 326, 390.

35 / As an example, see John D. Milligan, "The Treatment of an Historical Source," *History and Theory* 18 (1979): 177–96.

36 / *Collected Works of Lincoln* 3:399.

37 / LaWanda Cox, *Lincoln and Black Freedom: A Study in Presidential Leadership* (Columbia: University of South Carolina Press, 1981) 21–22.

38 / *Collected Works of Lincoln,* 1:114.

39 / Edmund Wilson, *Patriotic Gore: Studies in the Literature of the American Civil War* (New York: Oxford University Press, 1962), 106–8; George B. Forgie, *Patricide in the House Divided: A Psychological Interpretation of Lincoln and His Age* (New York: W. W. Norton and Co., 1979), 61–63, 84–87, and passim; Dwight G. Anderson, *Abraham Lincoln: The Quest for Immortality* (New York: Alfred A. Knopf, 1982), 68–78 and passim;

Strozier, *Lincoln's Quest for Union*, 59–61; James Hurt, "All the Living and the Dead: Lincoln's Imagery," *American Literature* 52 (1980–81): 364–68.

40 / Some two years later, in his speech on the subtreasury proposal, Lincoln referred to Democratic leaders as "oppressors," and to their party as the "evil spirit" reigning in Washington that constituted a threat to American liberties. *Collected Works of Lincoln* 1:178.

41 / Ibid., 5:388–89.

42 / *Congressional Globe,* 35th Cong., 1st sess., 18.

43 / Benjamin P. Thomas, *Abraham Lincoln* (New York: Alfred A. Knopf, 1952), 342.

44 / Albert Shaw, *Abraham Lincoln: The Year of His Election* (New York: Review of Reviews, 1929), 269.

45 / Michael Davis, *The Image of Lincoln in the South* (Knoxville: University of Tennessee Press, 1971), 82–83; *London Times,* October 21, 1862.

46 / Wilson, *Patriotic Gore,* 122, 639–41, 643–47.

47 / Charles N. Smiley, "Lincoln and Gorgias," *Classical Journal* 13 (1917–18): 125.

48 / Hurt, "All the Living and the Dead"; Theodore C. Blegen, *Lincoln's Imagery: A Study in Word Power* (La Crosse, Wis.: Sumac Press, 1954).

49 / Jacques Barzun, *Lincoln the Literary Genius* (Evanston, Ill.: Schori Private Press, 1960), 26, 36.

50 / *Collected Works of Lincoln,* 4:261–62 n, 271. For comparisons of the Seward and Lincoln versions of the paragraph, see Basler, *Touchstone for Greatness,* 99–100; Herbert J. Edwards and John E. Hankins, *Lincoln the Writer: The Development of His Literary Style* (Orono, Me.: University Press, 1962), 65–66.

WILLIAM E. GIENAPP

★

Who Voted for Lincoln?

ELECTION DAY 1860 DAWNED BRIGHT AND CLEAR ACROSS most of the North. Throughout the day, in rural hamlets and urban metropolises, in eastern communities and western settlements, party spokesmen importuned the undecided in the quest for last-minute converts, distributors pressed party tickets into the hands of supporters as they arrived to vote, and volunteers scoured the area for slackers and brought them to the polls. In some places the crush of voters was so great that men patiently waited in line for more than an hour before depositing their ballots. With only a few exceptions, balloting in the northern states passed quietly. As veteran politicians noted, despite the momentous consequences at stake, it was the calmest national election in forty years.[1]

Popular excitement was especially high in Springfield, the state capital nestled in the heart of the Illinois prairie and the home of Abraham Lincoln, the Republican candidate for president.[2] Zealous partisans commenced firing party cannons at sunrise to rouse the slumbering citizens, and discharges continued intermittently for several hours. Adding to the constant din, musical bands in wagons and on foot traveled about the town, blaring popular tunes and stirring up enthusiasm. By the time the polls opened, a large crowd had gathered at the courthouse and continued to mill about the square all day. Lincoln spent most of the day in his campaign office in the nearby state capitol, but in the afternoon, during a momentary lull, he walked over to the polls, where he was engulfed by a cheering throng of well-wishers. Patiently making his way through the multitude, and having already carefully cut his name and the presidential electors from the Republican ticket, he unceremoniously voted.

When the first returns began to arrive in midevening, Lincoln, joined by a handful of political associates, went down to the telegraph office in order to receive the results as soon as they came clattering over the wires. Throughout the evening, telegraphic dispatches brought news of Republican victories, first in his own state, soon swelling with returns from other western states. As the small group around the candidate talked and joked, all present anxiously awaited word from the East. By ten, reports indicated that Lincoln had carried Pennsylvania, but not until after midnight did telegrams arrive announcing the success of the Republican ticket in New York. Additional returns confirmed these earlier reports, and by 1:30 all doubt of Lincoln's election had been removed. Bidding good night to his associates, the president-elect walked quietly home alone, while back at the courthouse square exuberant Republicans broke into one of the most popular party songs of the now-concluded campaign, "Ain't you glad you joined the Republicans?"

THE IMPORTANCE of the 1860 presidential election needs no introduction. Certainly no election in our history precipitated such a serious national crisis or had such profound consequences. In response to the Republicans' first national triumph, the seven states of the Deep South seceded from the Union, and, six weeks after Lincoln took office, the Civil War began. By the time that Lincoln's presidency tragically came to an end, the Union had been preserved, slavery had been destroyed, and over 620,000 men had lost their lives.

In weighing the significance of the 1860 presidential election, historians have attributed markedly different meanings to the Republicans' success.[3] Over the years, they have interpreted it as a triumph of the forces of industrial capitalism, the result of the insistence that slavery no longer be allowed to expand and that, in Lincoln's words, it be put "in course of ultimate extinction," the product of an evangelical reform impulse bent on imposing cultural uniformity on the nation's out groups, and the culmination of a generation of reckless political agitation and overheated partisan propaganda. Manifesting a similar diversity of opinion concerning the causes of Lincoln's victory—a related but nevertheless distinct question—scholars have emphasized among other things the tariff issue, the homestead question, Northerners' moral hatred of slavery, the German vote, Lincoln's strength among Yankees and evangelicals, and the crippling divisions among the opposition. At least one student has argued that the campaign represented "intellectual chaos," and that the parties' attitudes on the major questions of the day were "so complex and obscure . . . that no clear mandate could possibly emerge from the election." Uncertain what to make of the election, Allan Nevins declared that "altogether, it was a very curious, a very mixed, and except for its grand central result, a very inscrutable election."[4]

These widely differing interpretations reflect several factors: the changing fashion of historical interpretation, the difficulty of correlating party propaganda with mass electoral behavior, the lack of sources on mass political attitudes, and the inherent ambiguity of the historical evidence for any event as complicated as a national election involving several million voters. But another problem that has contributed to historians' uncertainty concerning the 1860 election is that despite all the interpretations of the meaning of Lincoln's victory, we know little about the sources of his electoral support. Few systematic analyses of the Republican vote in 1860 have been done, and those available generally focus on a single community or at most on a single state.[5] Yet we can never comprehend the dynamics of this election and the reasons for its outcome unless we have a clearer idea of who voted for Lincoln. The make-up of the electoral coalition that put Abraham Lincoln in the White House remains one of the important unanswered questions of antebellum politics. Analysis of Lincoln's support can enhance our understanding of the nature of the early Republican party and the process by which a northern Republican majority crystallized in the 1860 presidential election.

It is only a slight exaggeration to say that the 1860 Republican presidential campaign began as soon as the 1856 national election was over. Though defeated, Republican managers were elated by their party's performance in the 1856 election, which far surpassed their most sanguine expectations six months earlier (table 1). The Republican party's second-place finish established its credentials as a viable political organization and destroyed the national aspirations of the rival Know-Nothing or American party. Lacking any claim to political distinction, John C. Frémont, the party's first presidential candidate, won a plurality of the northern vote over both James Buchanan and Millard Fillmore and in the process carried every northern state but five: New Jersey, Pennsylvania, Indiana, Illinois, and California. Had Frémont carried Pennsylvania and one other state that he lost, or had he carried the other four states without Pennsylvania, he would have been elected without any significant support in the South.

Nevertheless, Republicans still confronted a difficult challenge after the 1856 election. For one thing, as Horace Greeley pointed out, Frémont's popular image as a romantic adventurer brought him many votes, and thousands more were attributable to the emotional reaction to the caning of Senator Charles Sumner in May 1856. Greeley contended that Frémont's vote "considerably exceeded the solid strength, at that time, of the Republican party," which he put at no more than 1,200,000 votes after its first national campaign.[6] Equally troubling to party managers was that outside New England, Frémont secured a majority of the votes only in Michigan and Wisconsin. In the most heavily populated northern states—states that were essential for a Republican national victory—Frémont won less than 49 percent of the vote in Ohio, about 46 percent in New York, and slightly more than 40 percent in Indiana and Illinois (table 2). Even worse was his showing in Pennsylvania, where he garnered only 32 percent of the vote, and in New Jersey, where he secured 29 percent.

Republican managers realized that Frémont had been defeated because too many nativist Know-Nothings and conservative old-line Whigs voted for Fillmore. In general, these men were less concerned about the slavery issue, and many considered the Republican party a radical organization whose success would endanger the Union. The objective of Republicans during the next four years was clear: they had to retain the bulk of their previous supporters and at the same time broaden their political base in the North. Some Republican leaders, most notably Horace Greeley of the *New York Tribune* and Francis Preston Blair, Sr., believed that the party could establish a beachhead in the border slave states and eventually become a national rather than a sectional party, but Republican strategists realized that in the short run at least this goal was not realistic.[7] Republicans continued to confine their efforts to the free states, where the necessary accessions would have to be won.

Other than new voters, the most promising source of additional Republican votes was from the ranks of the American party. If, as most observers expected, the American organization continued to disintegrate, Republicans needed to win the bulk of its northern adherents. Of the approximately 400,000 votes Fillmore polled in the North, he won almost 165,000 in the five free states Frémont lost. Moreover, between them Frémont and Fillmore polled a majority of the votes in New Jersey, Illinois, and California, and they had only slightly less than that in Pennsylvania and Indiana. Fillmore's strength in the North was concentrated in eastern New York in the Hudson valley, in eastern Pennsylvania, especially Philadelphia and the surrounding area, in southernmost New Jersey and the region around Newark, and in the southern counties of Indiana and Illinois. In order to win in 1860, Republicans had to increase their vote in the lower North. As political observers easily foresaw, the so-called doubtful states—those northern states Frémont had failed to carry—held the key to the 1860 presidential election.

The Republican party's electoral fortunes oscillated after 1856, but despite an improved showing in 1858 following the Lecompton struggle in Congress, its position was not secure. Voter loyalties remained unstable, as evidenced by an unusual degree of shifting from one election to the next. In New York, the die-hard American element still held the balance of power, as the 1859 state election demonstrated, and Republicans had yet to establish their dominance in key states such as Pennsylvania, Indiana, and Illinois, which remained closely divided. Adding force to party managers' concern about the upcoming campaign were the spring elections in which the Republicans had not done as well as expected.[8] Throughout the early months of 1860, Republican politicans, with an eye to victory, intensely debated who should be the party's presidential nominee. These discussions inevitably returned to the critical problem of winning the doubtful states. One Iowa Republican expressed the prevailing point of view among party pragmatists concerning whom the party should nominate when he succinctly announced: "I am for the man who can carry Pennsylvania, New Jersey, and Indiana, with the reservation, that I will not go into cemetery or catacomb; the candidate must be alive, and able to walk at least from parlor to dining-room."[9]

These considerations weighed heavily on the delegates' minds when they gathered in Chicago in May 1860 for the party's national convention.[10] Western Republicans had manifested considerable concern earlier that Stephen A. Douglas, the expected Democratic nominee, would be a formidable opponent, but with the Democratic party apparently hopelessly split following the Charleston convention, a Republican victory seemed all but assured, providing the party adopted a sufficiently broad platform and selected the right candidate. "I want to succeed this time," Greeley wrote prior to the convention, "yet I know the country is not Anti-Slavery. It will only swallow a little Anti-Slavery in a great deal of sweetening. An Anti-Slavery man *per se* cannot be elected; but a Tariff, River-and-Harbor, Pacific Railroad, Free-Homestead man, *may* succeed *although* he is Anti-Slavery. . . . I mean to have as good a candidate as the majority will elect."[11] Greeley's concerns were shared by many other delegates. "Since the Democratic breaking up, the conviction had deepened that this party had the Presidency within reach," another member of the convention recalled. "The nearness of it made everybody uncommonly fearful of losing it."[12] A mood of caution tempered the proceedings.

The 1860 Republican platform was skillfully drafted to appeal to a wide segment of northern opinion. Without retreating from its opposition to the expansion of slavery, the party's statement of principles was more moderate than in 1856, when the Republican platform had focused almost exclusively on the slavery controversy. Whereas the 1856 platform denounced slavery as a "relic of barbarism," and insisted that it was not only the right but "the imperative duty of Congress" to prohibit the institution from all the territories, the 1860 document simply called for congressional exclusion of slavery from the territories "whenever such legislation is necessary," while pledging to preserve "inviolate . . . the right of each state to order and control its own domestic institutions." Following the rejection of the proslavery Lecompton constitution for Kansas, a number of party leaders believed that slavery could not expand into any of the existing territories, and therefore it would not be necessary for Congress to bar the institution. Further indicative of its moderation, the platform as originally reported contained only a general endorsement of the Declaration of Independence's promise of liberty and equality instead of a direct quotation as in 1856. Only a floor protest and brief walk-out by Joshua R. Giddings, an antislavery stalwart and one of the founders of the party in Ohio, restored the passage. It is true, as some historians have noted, that the conservative nature of the Republican platform's language on slavery can be exaggerated; after all, it should not be forgotten that 60 percent of the voters rejected the party in 1860, and that seven states left the Union almost immediately after its triumph. Nevertheless, both in its tone and program, the Republican platform in 1860 was more moderate than its predecessor.[13]

In a bid for the support of specific groups, the platform also incorporated several economic planks. As in 1856, it again urged federal aid for a transcontinental railroad, which along with a plank calling for daily overland-mail service was an appeal to the Pacific Coast states. The platform also demanded passage of a homestead law, which some thought would strengthen the party in the West, and endorsed river-and-harbor improvements with the Great Lakes states in mind. Finally, under strong pressure from the Pennsylvania delegation, the platform called for "such an adjustment of those imposts as to encourage the development of the industrial interests of the whole country." Designed to appease Pennsylvania without alienating former Democrats and western Republicans, many of whom held free-trade sentiments, this ambiguously worded pronouncement at most upheld a moderately protective tariff.[14]

Despite some squabbling over slavery and the tariff, the "most difficult" problem for party managers, as one delegate later declared, was to harmonize the Know-Nothings and foreign born.[15] And indeed the most controversial part of the platform was the fourteenth section, the so-called Dutch plank, put in at the behest of German Republicans, which opposed "any change in our naturalization laws or any state legislation by which the rights of citizenship hitherto accorded to immigrants from foreign lands shall be abridged or impaired." This declaration was a thinly veiled reference to the so-called Two Year Amendment in Massachusetts, which the voters had adopted in 1859 imposing a two-year waiting period for naturalized citizens before they could vote or hold office. Germans and antinativist Republicans had strongly protested against this amendment, and German leaders insisted that a disavowal of such legislation was essential if the Republicans were to win the German vote in the fall contest. The language was designed not to offend the Know-Nothings but was not entirely successful; several eastern Republicans hastened to urge that in accepting the nomination, Lincoln refrain from any specific endorsement of this section.[16]

Constructed to appeal to a wide segment of the northern electorate, the Republican platform represented the view of party leaders of what was needed to carry the election. So, too, did Lincoln's nomination. New York Senator William Henry Seward had been the frontrunner for the nomination, but Lincoln snared the prize on the third ballot. The Illinois leader possessed several advantages that contributed to his selection: he came from a doubtful state, he enjoyed a reputation as a moderate on the slavery issue, and he was acceptable to all party factions. In analyzing Lincoln's success, however, historians have not given sufficient emphasis to the importance of nativism in the party's membership and popular appeal. Seward had been an outspoken critic of the Know-Nothing party and for two decades had vigorously defended the rights of Catholics and immigrants. He had earned the undying enmity of the Know-Nothings, many of whom by now were affiliated with the Republican party, and Republican managers recognized that a sizable number of past and present Americans would not support the New York senator. "It is conceded by all judicious and well advised men," the chairman of the New Jersey delegation warned, "that Mr. Seward's Nomination will revive the divisions of 1856 in Pennsylvania and New Jersey, and will be fatal to us in those states." In referring to Seward's possible nomination, a Pennsylvania man bluntly proclaimed, "A nomination which will drive the Fillmore vote over to John Bell must necessarily prove fatal to the Republican ticket."[17] Moreover, the fourteenth section of the platform made it especially important that the nativist element in the party not be further alienated by the nomination. While despising the Know-Nothings' bigotry, Lincoln had restricted his criticism to private correspondence. At the same time, he had been careful to keep on good terms with German leaders in his state, and consequently he was acceptable to both groups. With an eye to victory, the delegates turned to Lincoln as the strongest candidate they could run in battleground states, where the outcome of the election would be determined. "It seems that Providence has taken care of us," commented Francis P. Blair, Jr., an anti-Seward man, in hailing Lincoln's selection.[18]

Republicans entered the campaign with their spirits high. The opposition was badly divided, for in addition to Bell on the Constitutional

Union ticket there were two Democratic candidates, Stephen A. Douglas, the representative of the northern wing of the party, and John C. Breckinridge of Kentucky, Buchanan's vice president, who was the candidate of most southern Democrats. Douglas was the strongest possible candidate a united Democratic party could have run, but as the nominee of only half of the party the Little Giant labored under insuperable disadvantages. The hostility of the Buchanan administration and southern Democrats dampened the spirits of Douglas's supporters, the presence of a Breckinridge ticket in the free states perpetuated the party division and ill feeling, and with such slim hopes of being elected, he was unable to raise campaign funds. The Republicans, on the other hand, displayed unusual unity and encountered much less trouble than in 1856 obtaining sufficient campaign contributions, and the prospect of victory brought in additional converts. A veteran of many national campaigns, James G. Blaine observed that "confidence of strength is as potential an element in a political canvass as in a military campaign," and recalled that Republicans' optimism in 1860 was "contagious" and soon "enveloped the free States."[19]

The Republican campaign in 1860 had three basic components. Republicans raised a wide variety of issues before the people; they gave considerable attention to Lincoln's personality and the symbolic qualities of his life story; and they resorted to political pageantry and other aspects of a hurrah campaign to rouse mass excitement.

While Republicans conducted a less narrowly focused campaign than they had in 1856, they continued to give first importance to the slavery issue, emphasizing as they had previously the Slave Power's threat to northern white liberties and the nation's republican heritage, and the danger that slavery expansion posed to the North's free-labor system.[20] Still, Republicans varied their campaign according to the region and tailored their appeal to attract specific groups. Thus in Pennsylvania and New Jersey, party spokesmen devoted great attention to the tariff; in the West, on the other hand, the homestead issue and internal improvements received considerable attention. To old Whigs, Republicans stressed Lincoln's Whig antecedents and his long support for Henry Clay, while among Germans they cited his opposition to the Massachusetts Two Year Amendment. At the same time that they courted the foreign born, Republicans confronted the ticklish situation of winning additional Know-Nothing support. As they had in the past, Republicans catered to anti-Catholic feeling, which was one sentiment that united nativists and Protestant immigrants. Seeking to exploit group hostilities and damn by association, Republican papers charged that Catholics represented Douglas's main source of support, and the Republican press devoted so much attention to the false accusation that Douglas, who had married a Catholic, had converted to the Roman faith that Democratic editors felt it necessary to issue a denial. The correspondence of the Republican National Committee reveals a very heavy demand for one-time Know-Nothings to address Republican meetings. Republicans also continued to nominate former Americans for important public and party offices. In New York, for example, they selected James O. Putnam, a former Know-Nothing legislator who had gained notoriety for successfully championing an anti-Catholic church-property law, to head their electoral ticket as one of the state's electors-at-large.

While Lincoln took no public role in the campaign, honoring the tradition that presidential candidates should not make stump speeches or issue official pronouncements, he was the inspiration for many of the symbols the party invoked, and he proved to be a strong candidate. Sensitive to the necessity of avoiding the aristocratic stigma that had so burdened the Whigs, Republican leaders quickly saw that Lincoln's image as "The Railsplitter" could be used to good advantage. Stressing his humble log-cabin birth, his hardscrabble rural childhood, his early life of toil and self-education, his folksy humor and unpretentious manners, Republican propagandists transformed Lincoln into a powerful symbol of democracy. He was, as one campaign biography declared, "a personification of the distinctive genius of our country and its institutions."[21] By fusing Lincoln with fundamental American values and myths, this popular image of him served to overcome Easterners' suspicions that the Republican candidate was "too much of a backwoodsman to fill and adorn" the presidency. This approach can be seen quite clearly in the *Philadelphia North American,* which described Lincoln as "a representative of that energetic . . . and progressive people, who have, by their own strong arms and stout hearts, cleared the forests, plowed the prairies, constructed the railroads and carried the churches and schoolhouses into the once wilderness . . . causing it to blossom like a garden, and diffusing blessings everywhere." He was, this organ of eastern conservativism affirmed, the personification of America's belief in progress and future greatness.[22]

The railsplitter idea originated with future Governor Richard J. Oglesby of Illinois, who arranged for Lincoln's cousin John Hanks to appear at the Republican state convention in early May with two fence rails he claimed to have split with Lincoln in 1830. The idea quickly caught on, and Oglesby operated something of a concession in Lincoln rails that summer.[23] Campaign papers in Chicago and Cincinnati appeared under the title *The Rail Splitter,* and political cartoons, party badges and stationery, and other campaign paraphernalia soon elevated the rail to an unofficial party symbol. Much like the Whigs' log cabin and hard cider campaign in 1840, the Republican campaign in 1860 skillfully exploited the populist symbols of the log cabin and the rail to appeal to ordinary voters. Testified one party worker: "It has also afforded me sincere pleasure to think of Mr. Lincoln taking possession of the White House; he, who was once the inmate of the log cabin—were he the pampered, effeminated child of fortune, no such pleasing emotions would be inspired."[24]

Political symbols, as has been widely noted, carry ideological meaning as well as evoke an emotional response, and those connected with Lincoln and his career effectively reinforced several Republican themes. As the embodiment of the log cabin to White House myth, Lincoln perfectly exemplified the party's free-labor ideal, which extolled the virtues of hard work, self-discipline, achievement, and social mobility. His humble origins and common touch also could easily be related to the party's attack on the Slave Power as an aristocracy that menaced the American principle of equality. Finally, his popular image as Honest Abe formed a particularly effective contrast to the sorry record of Buchanan, who presided over what was the most corrupt administration in the country's history to that point.[25] A Republican paper in Illinois affirmed that "*something* in his nature, in the constitution of his mind, in his personal appearance and manners, commends itself to the plain simplicity of the rural populations, and rouses in them an enthusiasm for his person and character such as no mere dogmas, however truthful, could ever strengthen."[26]

With Lincoln seemingly destined to win, Republican leaders relied on political pageantry to generate enthusiasm among the party faithful.[27] The most obvious manifestation of this aspect of the 1860 campaign was the famous Wide Awake Society, which attracted widespread attention. Originally founded in Hartford in February, the organization quickly spread throughout the North. Donning a uniform of glazed caps and oil-cloth capes and carrying torches attached to a rail, members marched to the accompaniment of martial music in military-like drill, chanting slogans, singing campaign songs, and cheering the party's candidates. Some clubs gained fame by perfecting a zigzag march in the shape of a rail fence. By the campaign's conclusion, observers estimated that several hundred thousand men belonged to the Wide-Awakes or similar Republican societies, such as the "Rail Splitters" and the "Rail Maulers." They brought a splash of color and excitement to a campaign that seemed to have a foreordained conclusion, and they left an indelible imprint on the memory of participants in the first Lincoln campaign.[28]

The significance of the Wide-Awakes, however, was greater than is generally recognized. For one thing, members were overwhelmingly young men; in fact, opponents charged, with some justification, that a number were too young to vote.[29] Such activity was a means of politicizing younger partisans who lacked firmly established party loyalties, of transmitting their enthusiasm to older residents of the community, and of giving younger party loyalists a sense of having contributed to the final result. Often mobilizing men who, as one Republican noted, in the past "never troubled themselves about politics except on Election days," the Wide-Awakes' political activities and party services extended well beyond the torchlight processions for which they were best known. The clubs were also "designed to cooperate in all the minutiae of political work," the *Chicago Democrat* reported, "and by arguments, documents, and all honorable means, to secure the wavering and persuade the hostile, acting as checkers, challengers, and patrolmen, bringing every vote to the polls."[30] More important, the Wide-Awakes were closely modeled on earlier Know-Nothing marching organizations, which had attracted young laborers, mechanics, and farm boys with their uniforms, quasi-military discipline, and social aspects; indeed, some American groups in 1856 had even used the name Wide-Awakes. Unlike the Know-Nothing lodges, the Wide-Awakes were not secret societies with special grips and passwords, but they did have regular weekly meetings, wore unique and often quite colorful uniforms, preserved carefully marked distinctions between officers and regular recruits (including different uniforms and even differently colored lanterns), and drew their membership from the same social classes.[31] To affiliates, the Wide-Awakes offered a chance to experience the camaraderie and excitement of a political marching society.

Republican prospects depended on the heavily populated and doubtful northern states. The state elections in mid-October in Pennsylvania, Ohio, and Indiana, in which the Republican state tickets were elected in all three states, gave unmistakable signs of an impending Republican triumph. In response, the opposition mounted a frantic campaign in New York to prevent Lincoln's election, and eventually the supporters of Douglas, Bell, and Breckinridge agreed on a common electoral ticket in a desperate effort to deny the state to Lincoln.[32] A less harmonious fusion was also worked out in Pennsylvania, but Republican leaders in both states nevertheless remained confident of victory. As the campaign drew to a close, Lincoln was the only candidate with any chance of being elected by the people. All hope of throwing the contest into the House of Representatives rested on the outside possibility that the united opposition could keep New York out of Lincoln's column.

The electorate rendered its decision on November 6. In the popular vote, Lincoln easily ran ahead of each of his three opponents, polling 1,865,000 votes, virtually all of which were cast in the North (table 1). The Republican total was a half million votes greater than in 1856. Lincoln won 54 percent of the northern vote, a gain of 8 percent over Frémont's share in 1856, and he carried every northern state except New Jersey, which he split with Douglas. In the nation as a whole, however, Lincoln trailed the combined opposition by almost one million votes and won less than 40 percent of the votes cast. Yet in the electoral college, the Republican nominee had 180 votes, 27 more than he needed to be elected. Moreover, as several scholars have noted, Lincoln would have won even if all the opposition votes had been combined. Only in New Jersey, California, and Oregon did Lincoln's margin of victory result from the division of the opposition vote, and these states provided him with only 11 electoral votes.

That a northern sectional party could win a national election with a minority of the popular vote was hardly a new revelation. The most significant fact of the election was not that Lincoln won because of the way that the electoral college operates, but that he carried every northern state except one, and that he won the important doubtful states of

Pennsylvania, Indiana, and Illinois.[33] Lincoln picked up additional votes precisely where he most needed them. His percentage declined compared to Frémont's only in Maine, Massachusetts, and Vermont, all of which were safely Republican, whereas in the eight states in which Frémont lacked a majority, Lincoln's average increase was 12 percent, and in the key state of Pennsylvania, his proportion was a staggering 24 percent higher (table 2).

Despite widespread reports of a lack of excitement during the campaign, voter turnout in 1860 was high. Elsewhere I have estimated that in the free states 82 percent of the eligible voters went to the polls, a figure that is conservative and understates the true turnout.[34] This rate of participation exceeded that in the presidential elections of 1848 and 1852, and it was less than 1 percent below that of the stirring 1856 campaign. Overall, the Democrats were only slightly less successful than the Republicans in retaining their traditional supporters (87 to 84 percent respectively), and in New York, Ohio, and Illinois, the Democrats actually enjoyed a slight advantage (tables 3–11).[35] Besides their traditional hostility toward Republicans, Douglas men had the added incentive of wanting to preserve their state organizations.

It was the 1856 American voters—not the Democrats—who evidenced a high rate of nonvoting and massive defections to other parties. The extent of nonvoting among former Americans no doubt reflected a dislike of both the Republicans and Democrats along with a belief that Bell's cause was hopeless. One former American in Indiana indicated that he preferred Bell but added, "I did not vote in the presidential election from the fact that my vote in this State would amount to nothing." Bell leaders testified that one of the greatest handicaps they encountered was the widespread conviction among potential supporters that Bell could not win. Other Fillmore Americans chose the lesser of two evils and switched to another party rather than throw away their vote. In endorsing Lincoln, the *Buffalo Commercial Advertiser,* Fillmore's former personal organ, gave as one of its reasons "the knowledge of the little strength belonging to John Bell in this State."[36]

Northern Democrats contended afterwards that their defeat was the result of the disruption of the party at Charleston. "Our break up there," one New York City Democrat typically asserted, "elected Mr Lincoln."[37] In his usual brash manner, Douglas boasted afterwards that backed by a united party he would have beaten Lincoln in every northern state except Vermont and Massachusetts. Northern voting patterns, however, raise strong doubts that the Democrats could have prevailed even had they been united. In reality, Democratic apathy was not a decisive factor on the outcome in any of the nine states under scrutiny. Despite the apparent hopelessness of their cause, Democrats were more adept than the Republicans in getting out their traditional vote in Connecticut, Illinois, Maine, Massachusetts, and Pennsylvania, and their advantage was quite substantial in Connecticut and Massachusetts. In the remaining states, a larger proportion of Republicans went to the polls, but in none of them was Lincoln's edge significant. In addition, Republican claims that "*life long* Democrats are by scores voting [*sic*] for the Lincoln ticket" were greatly exaggerated.[38] Democrats, in fact, were remarkably successful in retaining their usual supporters: only in Pennsylvania did many traditional Democrats go over to the Republicans, and Alexander K. McClure, the Republican state chairman, was undoubtedly correct that the bulk of these Democratic bolters were Douglas men alienated by the creation of a fusion electoral ticket in the state.[39] Moreover, in several states, most notably New York and to a lesser extent Connecticut, Democratic accessions from Frémont voters exceeded their loss of past supporters. Douglas's defeats in the pivotal states of New York, Pennsylvania, Indiana, and Illinois were not attributable to traditional Democrats staying home on election day, defecting to the Republicans, or throwing away their votes on Bell or Breckinridge. Rather, it was among former Americans, nonvoters, and new voters that Douglas was at a disadvantage. Had the Democratic party not divided, it seems all but certain that the only additional free states Douglas would have carried were California, Oregon, and the four electors he lost in New Jersey.[40]

The October state elections in Pennsylvania, Ohio, and Indiana—three crucial states—cast additional doubt on the importance of the Democratic split in Lincoln's victory. In all three states, Democrats united on a single ticket, and the Constitutional Union party did not make any state nominations. Although the state contests were closer, the Republicans won clear majorities in all three states, and only in Pennsylvania was there any significant falling off in the Democratic total vote in the presidential election.[41] Indeed, the behavior of the 1856 Buchanan voters was strikingly similar in the state and presidential elections (tables 12–14). Democratic abstentions were not significantly different in November compared to October, and the rate of Democratic defections to the Republicans was also approximately the same; in fact, Ohio Democrats actually were more successful in holding their traditional supporters in November than in the state election.[42] Except for Pennsylvania, the Democratic setbacks in October and the continuing division between Breckinridge and Douglas also do not seem to have caused voters with less established partisan loyalties to desert the Democratic party or not vote.[43] In short, mass voting patterns in 1860 provide no evidence that the outcome of the presidential election would have been any different if the Democracy had not ruptured at Charleston.

Lincoln by and large retained the support of men who backed Frémont four years earlier. He also obtained the votes of many men who did not vote in 1856 (either because of age or other disqualifications or from lack of interest), especially in the rapidly growing western states. Outside of New England, however, Douglas also won substantial numbers of new voters and former abstainers, and Lincoln's advantage was not very large except in Illinois. Douglas actually did slightly better than Lincoln among such voters in Pennsylvania (tables 3–11).

The most important gains Lincoln made over Frémont occurred among former Know-Nothings and conservatives who voted for Fillmore in 1856. Republican party workers reported significant accessions among the Fillmore men as the campaign progressed. "We are fast gaining ground out West," Lincoln's law partner William Herndon confidently noted. "The 'old line Whigs' are . . . going almost unanimously and wildly for Lincoln." A New York correspondent informed Lincoln that the Americans "are in fellowship with us in the rural districts, & I found a much stronger inclination towards affiliation in the City, than has been supposed."[44] These reports were not without foundation. Lincoln won 40 percent or more of the Fillmore vote in Indiana and Ohio; over 50 percent in New York; over 60 percent in Iowa; better than 70 percent in Illinois; and over 80 percent in Pennsylvania (tables 3–11). Although the Constitutional Union party upheld the Whig tradition of a national conservative party, only in Maine and Massachusetts did Bell win a larger proportion of Fillmore voters than Lincoln, but both were solidly Republican in any event, and in Connecticut, where the two men's support was almost equal, Democratic divisions made the state safe for Lincoln. American converts were crucial to the Republican victories in the doubtful states of Indiana, Illinois, and Pennsylvania, all of which Frémont lost, as well as the battleground state of New York, and consequently they were a vital component in Lincoln's winning coalition.[45]

Republican strength among these former Americans and old-line Whigs reflected several considerations. Lincoln was an old Whig, the Republicans had actively courted die-hard Americans by endorsing cherished nativist reforms in various states, the national platform was more moderate on the slavery issue and included several Whig economic planks, Republicans accorded former Americans places of honor in the campaign, and many were disgusted by the corrupt scandals of the Buchanan administration and the attempt to force the Lecompton constitution on the settlers of Kansas. Also important was their continuing hatred of the Democratic party and their belief that Bell could not win. Some who voted for Lincoln undoubtedly preferred Bell but felt that his cause was hopeless. One of Bell's New Jersey managers acknowledged that there were many conservatives who *"hate"* the Democrats but wanted "to see more signs of success for [Bell] to keep them from voting the Republican ticket." Another political observer described precisely the phenomenon operating among countless former Fillmore voters. "Men in a Presidential contest have a great desire to make their votes count for something besides *mere principles,"* he sadly noted, "& so will almost always cast them for some candidate who has a *possible* chance of election. If their *favorite* seems to have no chance whatever," he continued, "they will vote for him whom they think to be the 'next best man.'"[46] Many who continued to harbor strong animosity toward the Democrats gravitated to the Republican camp. After the election, a Bell man wrote that "thousands of men voted for Mr. Lincoln not that they admired particularly his principles but [from] the inveterate hatred they entertained toward the democratic party." In announcing its support for Lincoln, the *Buffalo Commercial Advertiser* referred to "the Old Whig hatred of Democracy, nursed in with our mother's milk, and strong today as in 1844."[47]

Lincoln received his greatest support in regions that had strongly backed Frémont, such as the Burned-Over District of western New York, the Northern Tier and western counties of Pennsylvania, Ohio's Western Reserve, and the northern counties of Indiana and Illinois. He did much better than Frémont, however, in areas where Fillmore had made a strong showing. Thus in the southern counties of Indiana, Lincoln almost doubled Frémont's proportion of the vote, and in southern Illinois his share of the vote represented a 2½-fold increase over 1856. At the same time, Bell did much worse than Fillmore in the North. Whereas Fillmore won 21 percent in southern Indiana and 27 percent in southern Illinois, Bell's vote dropped to less than 4 percent in both regions. Put another way, Bell's share of the total vote was less than one-eighth what Fillmore had won in southern Illinois, and less than one-fifth in southern Indiana (table 15).

These voting patterns provide important evidence concerning whether Seward, had he secured the Republican nomination, could have been elected.[48] Lincoln, as has been noted, won the nomination in large measure because of the belief that Seward could not carry the doubtful states. But was this fear, which was so evident among the delegates at Chicago, in fact well founded? Lincoln's margin of victory was relatively narrow in Illinois, where he led Douglas by 13,000 votes and the combined opposition by only 6,000 votes, and in Indiana, where his advantage was 23,000 votes over Douglas, and 6,000 over the combined opposition. In addition, his victories in California, Oregon, and part of New Jersey were by plurality, and he led his closest competitor in California by only 1,000 votes, and in New Jersey, his four electors prevailed by only 5,000 votes over the non-Douglas electors who were defeated. Moreover, while Lincoln's advantage in Pennsylvania was quite large (70,000 votes), the state election in October, when the Republican majority was about 22,000 votes, was a truer indication of each party's strength in the state. In Pennsylvania, Indiana, Illinois, and New York, Lincoln's victory stemmed in part from his support from Fillmore Americans, and without question Seward would not have run as well among these voters. Since Lincoln's majority was not large in Indiana or Illinois, any sizable defections among the Fillmore men would have cost him these states. Seward might have carried Pennsylvania in any case though with a smaller vote than Lincoln, and the same might have been true in New York, where the bitter animosity between the Seward and Fillmore factions had festered for more than a decade. But even in these states, the Republican majority was not unassailable. Assuming no other change in the vote distribution, if only half of Lincoln's American supporters in Pennsylvania and slightly more than a third in New York had gone over to the Fusion ticket, the Republicans would have lost both states. Such shifts certainly were not impossible had Seward been the Republican nominee. The New York senator counted on gaining additional support among immigrants to compensate for the nativist votes he would inevitably lose, but one Republican journalist accurately observed that "in [New York] city there never was a day when Seward could rely upon the 'foreign vote,' which he expected, to compensate for the American defection [in the rural districts]. That vote is driven to the polls like sheep to the shambles. A black one here & there might have been caught, but no more."[49] Although a weaker candidate than Lincoln, Seward would have finished first in the electoral college, but whether he would have had a majority is by no means certain, and had the election gone to the House, no one could guess what the outcome would be.[50] Legitimate reasons existed, in other words, for Republican delegates to doubt whether Seward could be elected, and on balance these fears seem justified.

Whatever the Republican party's image in the post–Civil War era as the party of big business, Lincoln's strength was concentrated in the countryside rather than in urban centers. Of the eleven cities in the North with populations over 50,000, Lincoln failed to win a majority in seven. Of the very largest cities (those with a population of over 100,000), Lincoln's best showing was in Chicago (59 percent), his poorest in New York City (35 percent).[51] Moreover, throughout the North, as correlation analysis confirms, Republican strength tended to increase in more rural areas. As one New York Democratic congressman admitted, "We have been, as it were, driven to take refuge within the walls of our northern cities."[52]

Several factors contributed to this situation. One was the strong opposition of the business community in some metropolitan areas to the Republican party, which they feared would disrupt southern trade and threaten the existence of the Union. Republican fundraisers testified that businessmen's hostility had lessened since 1856, when they were unable to raise much money in commercial centers other than Boston, but party leaders also reported that the commercial men were the mainstay of the Constitutional Union movement.[53] Businessmen had money and prestige but represented only a small number of votes. More important in explaining the Republicans' weakness in large cities was the hostility of many urban immigrants to the Republican party; in some cities, such as New York and Cincinnati, the foreign born constituted a majority of the population. Although Republicans sought immigrant support with conspicuous ardor during this decade, many of the foreign born, particularly those who were Catholic, continued to oppose the party. Republicanism was especially weak in cities with a large Irish-Catholic population, such as Boston and New York. Those with an effective Republican organization tended to contain a greater proportion of Protestant immigrants, such as Chicago, where many Germans settled, and Philadelphia, with its important Scotch-Irish community. "The strength of our opponents lies mainly in the populous cities," German leader Carl Schurz asserted, "and consists largely of the Irish and uneducated mass of German immigrants."[54]

Comments identifying Republicanism with the rural areas of the North and with farmers in particular are fairly common in Republican sources.[55] Occupational data for two states at the opposite ends of the country, Maine and Iowa, help clarify the relationship between occupation and voting in 1860 (table 16). In Maine, Republicans garnered a much larger share of farmers than the Democrats (36 to 16 percent), but among manufacturing workers, the division was approximately equal. In Iowa, a heavily agricultural state, the Republicans' advantage among farmers was very slight. Lincoln enjoyed a more pronounced advantage among skilled workers, while his opponents had a clear but not overwhelming edge among unskilled workers (28 to 37 percent).

The occupational basis of partisan allegiance can be clarified further by examining voting in 1860 in Cincinnati, Ohio, a large urban complex with a significant immigrant population (largely German) and considerable industry, and Chautauqua County, New York, located in the far western part of the state along Lake Erie (table 16). Chautauqua was an overwhelmingly rural county, with no important industry and only a few towns of any size, none of which approached being a city. Lincoln carried Cincinnati by a plurality, whereas Chautauqua, a Republican stronghold, gave Lincoln almost 70 percent of its vote.

In Cincinnati, unskilled laborers overwhelmingly gravitated to the Democratic party, and the Republican party had almost no support among this group. Among skilled workers, on the other hand, many of whom were native and not foreign born, Republicans did significantly better than the Democrats (56 to 29 percent). In Chautauqua County,

Lincoln's majority rested very heavily on his commanding majority among farmers; he won over four times as many of their votes as did the Fusion ticket. His margin was much less pronounced among workers and other groups.

The Republican party's self-projected image as the party of morality and uplift, along with its emphasis on free labor and economic achievement, no doubt strengthened it among farmers and rural voters, as well as skilled urban workers who were rising socially (or at least expected to). "Who form the strength of this party?" the *Springfield Republican* rhetorically asked:

> Precisely those who would most naturally be expected to—the great middling-interest class. The highest class, aristocratically associated and affiliated, timid, afraid of change, and holding in their hands the sensitive cords of commerce, and the lowest class, ignorant, deceived with a name, fed by the rich man's money, and led by the rich man's finger,—these are the forces arrayed against Republicanism, as a whole. . . . Those who work with their own hands, who live and act independently, who hold the stakes of home and family, of farm and workshop, of education and freedom—these, as a mass, are enrolled in the Republican ranks.[56]

While such self-congratulatory pronouncements were propaganda, they also accurately depicted the party's self-image during this decade.

Party leaders insisted at the Chicago convention that a broad platform that included several economic planks was essential if the party were to win in November, and the platform endorsed a homestead law in a direct appeal for western votes. Western Republicans placed heavy stress on the importance of the homestead issue in the election. "This Homestead measure overshadows everything with us, and through the West," a Minnesota man told Simon Cameron, and after the election Owen Lovejoy, a staunch antislavery congressman from Illinois, claimed that if the party had not endorsed a homestead law, "the Republicans never could have elected their President."[57] Adopting this line of argument, Allan Nevins argued that "without the homestead issue . . . the Republicans would doubtless have lost important States."[58] Voting patterns, however, cast doubt on the idea that the cry of free farms played a decisive role in Lincoln's election. Of the four westernmost free states that would have received the greatest benefit from a homestead law, the Republicans carried only two in 1860 by clear majorities (Iowa and Minnesota). In California and Oregon, where Lincoln managed to poll only about one-third of the votes, he ran behind his northern average by almost twenty points. Nor did Lincoln's victory in Iowa stem from a commanding majority among farmers; in fact, the Republicans' edge among farmers was greater in Maine than in Iowa, which is hardly consistent with the idea that the homestead issue had a decisive impact on Westerners' partisan loyalties (table 16). In addition, while party lines held fairly tightly in 1860, what gains Lincoln made among one-time Democrats occurred in the East rather than the West. Virtually none of Buchanan's supporters in 1856 defected to Lincoln in Ohio, Indiana, Illinois, or Iowa (tables 3–11).

Eastern Republicans, on the other hand, emphasized the role of the tariff issue in Lincoln's triumph, especially in Pennsylvania. While conceding that probably a majority of Lincoln's votes were not influenced by the tariff issue, James G. Blaine nevertheless insisted that it had "a controlling influence" in Pennsylvania (a view also endorsed by Cameron), and therefore was responsible for Lincoln's victory.[59] On the defensive on the slavery and race issues and anxious to appeal to old-line conservative Whigs, Pennsylvania Republicans seized on the tariff issue and gave it great emphasis. From that state one Democrat complained to Stephen A. Douglas in frustration that "the Republicans, in their speeches, say nothing of the nigger question, but all is made to turn on the Tariff," and the Republican *Philadelphia North American*, an ardent advocate of protectionism, insisted that "slavery was not the dominating idea in the Presidential contest."[60] It is difficult to weigh the influence of the tariff issue on Pennsylvania voting, because no direct index of protariff sentiment is available. Per capita industrial capitalization had a fairly strong *negative* influence on Lincoln's vote in the state once ethnicity, religion, and wealth are controlled, and Lincoln actually ran better in areas with greater household manufacturing than in urban industrial centers. Perhaps a better test is the proportion of iron workers in the population, since Republicans specifically defended the tariff as a means to promote the iron industry, which was so crucial to the state's economy. Again, independent of other variables the influence of this factor on the Republican vote was very slight.[61] While the tariff issue probably won some converts among former Whigs, it does not seem to have produced substantial defections to the

Republicans. The Republicans' new-found power in the state was directly traceable to the infusion of former Know-Nothings into the People's party organization, an influx that began before the party adopted its mild 1860 tariff plank. Nor was Pennsylvania, in the end, essential to Lincoln's victory, because he would have been elected without the state, thanks to the Democratic divisions in New Jersey, Oregon, and California.[62] Like the homestead plank, the tariff question has been overemphasized as a factor in mass voting behavior in the 1860 presidential election.

Since the 1950s, historians have increasingly challenged the view that party lines in the antebellum period closely mirrored economic divisions in society. In general, Republicanism displayed a positive relationship with per capita wealth, yet religion and ethnicity consistently overshadowed wealth as an influence on the Republican vote (tables 19–25).[63] In Ohio, which had a mixed agricultural and industrial economy, and which compiled an unusually good set of statistics on taxable property in the state in the 1850s, no strong connection existed between wealth and Republican strength. Commercial wealth of various types had mostly a weak negative relationship to Lincoln's vote in 1860 (i.e., the richer the area, the lower the Republican percentage). For indices of agricultural wealth, this relationship was often positive, but nonetheless weak.[64] On an individual level, however, wealth may have exerted greater influence. In Cincinnati, Lincoln won the least support from the very richest and very poorest groups in the city and did much better among voters whose wealth ranked them nearer the middle of society, a relationship that was probably typical for urban areas though perhaps not for rural communities. Lincoln was particularly weak among the propertyless class in the city, as the figures on voting for unskilled workers given earlier would suggest.

Republican leaders devoted much attention in 1860 to immigrant voters, and after the election some political observers claimed that the German vote, in particular, had been critical in the party's victory in many states. "In Ohio, Illinois, Indiana, Iowa, and Wisconsin," the *New York Herald* reported, "native Republicans now openly acknowledge that their victory was, if not wholly, at least to a great extent, due to the large accessions they received in the most hotly contested sections from the German ranks."[65] No aspect of voting behavior in the 1860 election has received greater attention from historians, and the argument has raged for years over whether the Germans voted for Lincoln.[66] Voting patterns confirm that Lincoln did better than Frémont among the foreign born, but that by no means did he garner an overwhelming proportion of naturalized voters. Among Germans, upon whom the Republicans lavished particular attention, Lincoln scored significant gains in Iowa, New York, and Pennsylvania—three of the four states for which data is available. Only in Ohio did he fail to improve on Frémont's showing, but even so Lincoln won a greater proportion of the German vote in that state (43 percent) than elsewhere (table 17). In terms of the election's outcome, Lincoln's most important increase among Germans was in Pennsylvania; 44 percent of the Pennsylvania Dutch voted for Lincoln, compared to only 3 percent who backed Frémont.[67] When other factors such as wealth and religion are controlled, the proportion of the population born in Germany did not significantly contribute to Lincoln's strength, and in Ohio and Indiana the relationship was strongly negative (tables 19–24).

Although German support for the Republican party apparently increased as the decade progressed, by the time of Lincoln's election the German community still remained deeply divided politically. In general, immigrant voters tended to divide along religious lines, with Protestants more likely to vote Republican and their Catholic countrymen to remain solidly Democratic (tables 19–24).[68] Such behavior is not surprising, given the Republican party's anti-Catholic image and the presence of so many Know-Nothings in the party's ranks. Protestant immigrants, including Germans, were hardly unanimous in their support of the Republican party, however, and, at least in New York and Ohio, the more evangelical German Reformed showed a greater affinity for the Republican party than the more conservative Lutherans, who no doubt were less comfortable with the party's moral reformist attitudes. Although some party members reported that German Democrats converted to the Republican cause, Lincoln's gains, at least in the West where Democratic defections were slight, probably came more from newly naturalized and younger immigrants than from their older countrymen with longer political involvement and stronger ties to the Democratic party.[69] Contemporaries reported strong support for the Republican party among Scandinavian, Dutch, and British immigrants, and voting patterns would seem to lend credence to such assertions, although not consistently in all states.[70] Few if any groups, on the other hand, were as strongly anti-Republican as Irish Catholics. No group came in for greater abuse and ridicule in the Republican press, and Republicans went out of their way to praise the Germans in comparison. Indeed, it seems likely, although precise data is lacking, that German Catholics were not as hostile to Lincoln as their Irish co-religionists. The Protestant Irish, in contrast, appear to have voted overwhelmingly Republican (the estimate for Pennsylvania, based on data for about one-third of the state's counties, exceeds 100 percent).

The Republican party had always been strong among native-born voters, and the substantial movement of Fillmore Americans into the party's ranks after 1856 increased its share of the native-born vote. Among those who voted, Lincoln won a clear majority of the native born in New York, Iowa, and Indiana. Yet if Lincoln did well among the native born, regional identifications were an important modifying influence. Contemporaries called attention to the powerful support rendered by New Englanders and their descendants in other states to the Republican party. Lincoln, in fact, swept the New England states (as had Frémont), but more revealing were the large majorities he received in Yankee-settled areas such as western New York, the Northern Tier of Pennsylvania, the Western Reserve of Ohio, and the northern counties of Indiana, Illinois, and Iowa. At the same time, pro-Republican sentiment was much weaker among residents of the free states who had come from the South. When factors such as religion and wealth are controlled, Yankees and Southerners displayed sharply contrasting partisanship. In fact, Yankees were the backbone of the party in New York, Ohio, Pennsylvania, and Indiana, as the geographic basis of voting in those states would suggest (tables 19–24). The sneers in the Republican press at southern culture, habits, and values, Republican spokesmen's constant boasting of northern superiority, and the party's exploitation of antisouthern feeling in the North understandably alienated former Southerners. The hostility of southern-born voters to the Republican party diminished somewhat by the end of the decade—Lincoln, of course, had been born in the South—but it was never eradicated before the war. After the 1860 election, the *Illinois State Journal* contended that a number of southern-born former Whigs had crossed over to the Republican party, and Lincoln apparently won many more votes among transplanted Southerners than had Frémont, but even with these accessions, the bulk of these voters continued to oppose the Republican party.[71] Lincoln won only about a third of southern-born voters in Indiana, and in Iowa he garnered almost none of their votes (table 18).[72]

In analyzing the nature of the early Republican party, some historians have argued that there was a strong religious basis to the party's support, and that in particular evangelical Protestants (Methodists, Baptists, Presbyterians, and Congregationalists), with their well-known affinity for moral reform, voted solidly Republican. Nonevangelical church groups, on the other hand, such as Episcopalians, Lutherans, and Catholics, allegedly voted Democratic in reaction to evangelicals' efforts to use the power of the state to control personal behavior.[73] That the Catholic vote was overwhelmingly Democratic seems clear. Partisan loyalties among Protestants, however, are much more difficult to generalize about. Some of the recent historical literature greatly exaggerates the uniformity of Protestant sects' political behavior from one state to another, as well as the level of support for the Republican party among evangelical church groups. Episcopalians seem to have opposed the party fairly strongly (which is consistent with the party's lack of support among the wealthiest groups in society), whereas the Quakers, with their strong antislavery tradition, were overwhelmingly Republican. However, among the Baptists, Methodists, and Presbyterians— the largest Protestant denominations in the North—no consistent pattern of party preference prevailed, although of the three groups the Presbyterians apparently were the most strongly Republican and the Methodists, the most evangelical church in America, the least so.[74] Perhaps indicative of their disparate make-up, the Baptists displayed no clear pattern of behavior, although contemporaries were probably right that the strongly evangelical, antislavery Free Will Baptists were largely Republican (table 24).[75] Republican strength among evangelicals seems to have increased during the decade, but at no point before the war did these groups form a monolithic voting bloc. Instead, large numbers of these voters—particularly Methodists and, in some localities, Baptists as well—continued to adhere to the Democratic party throughout the decade.

Observers of the 1860 campaign often pointed to the prominence of young men in the Republican ranks, and Seward in one of his rhetorical flourishes referred to it as "a party chiefly of young men." John Z. Goodrich, the Republican national committeeman from Massachusetts, reported after a fact-finding visit to Indiana that "more than three fourths of the young men who are now to vote the first time, are Republicans."[76] Because age was related to occupation, wealth, and ethnicity (a higher proportion of immigrants being young males), it is very difficult to determine the extent to which younger men backed Lincoln. Lincoln's support from new voters (most of whom were native born), however, lends credence to contemporary assertions that he displayed unusual strength among voters under twenty-five, virtually all of whom were casting their first presidential ballot in 1860. Douglas's strength among these voters may have been primarily from recently naturalized voters rather than from native-born citizens reaching adulthood, although, as noted above, Lincoln probably won a number of younger immigrants as well. Voters in the nineteenth century normally manifested strong partisan loyalties, and as is true with the modern electorate, this party identity grew stronger with age. Voting for the same party over a series of elections inevitably strengthened the psychological bond between a voter and his party. Thus it was exceedingly difficult—indeed almost impossible—to get antebellum voters to switch parties. Even in the wake of the Anti-Nebraska and Know-Nothing upheavals of mid-decade, most Democrats remained loyal to their party, or defected for no more than one or two elections before returning to their traditional loyalty. Younger voters, with weaker partisan identities, were more susceptible to changing parties or adopting a different affiliation than their family.[77] Young men were probably attracted to the Republican cause for a variety of reasons: the party's fresh and youthful spirit, the persuasiveness of its appeal, and the Democratic party's image as a tired, badly divided, and hopelessly corrupt organization. In this regard, the importance of the Wide-Awakes in strengthening the Republican party among younger voters should not be overlooked.

The question, Who elected Lincoln? does not lend itself to any precise answer. Obviously, every vote counted as much as any other vote in a state toward Lincoln's victory. As contemporary observers recognized, the Republican party was a diverse coalition, and many groups contributed to its first national victory. Three aspects of northern voting behavior after 1856, however, deserve particular emphasis. First, the growing support of non-Catholic immigrants for the Republican party was important, particularly because many had previously voted Democratic or normally would have after they were naturalized. Second, the Republicans' victory in 1860 also stemmed from the party's disproportionate strength among younger native-born voters. Just as in the 1930s, so in the 1850s the political realignment seems to have occurred less from older voters changing parties than from one party winning a preponderance of younger voters. Finally, the overwhelming backing Lincoln won among former Know-Nothings was perhaps the most important shift that produced his victory. Together, these changes in voting behavior led to the creation of a northern Republican majority in 1860 and to the election of Abraham Lincoln as the nation's first Republican president.

Table 1 / The Popular Vote for President

	Free States	Slave States	Total	Electoral Vote
		1856		
Frémont	1,339,341	1,194	1,340,535	114
Buchanan	1,226,105	606,850	1,832,955	174
Fillmore	405,246	466,485	871,731	8
		1860		
Lincoln	1,839,205	26,388	1,865,593	180
Opposition to Lincoln	1,572,637	1,248,520	2,821,157	
Fusion	580,426	15,420	595,846	
Douglas	815,857	163,568	979,425	12
Breckinridge	99,381	570,091	669,472	72
Bell	76,973	499,441	576,414	39

Adapted from Walter Dean Burnham, *Presidential Ballots, 1836–1892* (Baltimore, 1955), and the *Tribune Almanac* for 1857 and 1861. A precise breakdown of the Fusion vote is not possible, but Horace Greeley estimated that Douglas's supporters cast approximately 85 percent of these ballots (*American Conflict*, 1:328).

Table 2 / Republican Vote for President in 1856 and 1860: Northern States

	Frémont No.	Frémont %	Lincoln No.	Lincoln %	% Republican Gain
California	20,695	18.8	38,667	32.3	+13.5
Connecticut	43,077	53.4	43,488	54.1	+ 0.7
Illinois	96,158	40.2	171,313	50.8	+10.6
Indiana	94,378	40.1	139,033	51.1	+11.0
Iowa	43,954	49.1	70,406	54.9	+ 5.8
Maine	67,179	63.1	62,811	62.3	− 0.8
Massachusetts	108,190	64.8	106,533	63.0	− 1.8
Michigan	71,766	57.2	88,450	57.2	0
Minnesota	–	–	22,070	63.4	–
New Hampshire	37,473	53.7	37,519	56.9	+ 3.2
New Jersey	28,339	28.4	58,234	48.1	+19.7
New York	276,007	46.3	362,646	53.6	+ 7.3
Ohio	187,497	48.5	231,709	52.3	+ 3.8
Oregon	–	–	5,006	36.0	–
Pennsylvania	147,510	32.0	268,036	56.3	+24.3
Rhode Island	11,467	57.8	12,244	61.4	+ 3.6
Vermont	39,561	78.1	33,808	75.7	− 2.4
Wisconsin	66,090	55.3	86,110	56.6	+ 1.3
TOTAL NORTH		45.1		53.9	+ 8.8

TABLES 3–11 / ESTIMATED PROPORTIONS BETWEEN VOTING FOR
PRESIDENT 1856 AND PRESIDENT 1860

Table 3 / Maine

	Party in 1860					
Party in 1856	Republican	Douglas Democrat	Breckinridge Democrat	Constitutional Union	Not Voting	% Electorate 1860
Republican	34	1	1	0	5	40
Democrat	2	15	3	0	3	24
American	0	1	0	1	0	2
Not Eligible	2	1	0	0	4	7
Not Voting	0	−1	1	0	27	27
% Electorate 1860	38	18	4	1	39	

N = 377 townships

Table 4 / Massachusetts

	Party in 1860					
Party in 1856	Republican	Douglas Democrat	Breckinridge Democrat	Constitutional Union	Not Voting	% Electorate 1860
Republican	39	4	0	−1	6	48
Democrat	3	10	2	3	−1	16
American	3	3	0	7	−2	10
Not Eligible	2	1	0	1	4	8
Not Voting	2	−2	1	1	17	18
% Electorate 1860	48	15	3	10	24	

N = 321 townships

Table 5 / Connecticut

	Party in 1860						
Party in 1856	Republican	Douglas Democrat	Breckinridge Democrat	Constitutional Union	Fusion	Not Voting	% Electorate 1860
Republican	38	6	−7	−1	−2	10	44
Democrat	3	9	21	1	3	−1	36
American	2	−1	1	2	2	−2	3
Not Eligible	2	2	1	0	0	3	7
Not Voting	1	0	0	0	0	8	9
% Electorate 1860	46	16	16	2	2	18	

N = 146 townships

Table 6 / New York

	Party in 1860			
Party in 1856	Republican	Fusion	Not Voting	% Electorate 1860
Republican	36	5	−3	37
Democrat	−1	27	1	26
American	10	8	−1	17
Not Eligible	6	3	1	10
Not Voting	−2	0	11	10
% Electorate 1860	49	42	9	

N = 60 counties

Table 7 / Pennsylvania

Party in 1856	Party in 1860					
	Republican	Douglas Democrat	Fusion	Constitutional Union	Not Voting	% Electorate 1860
Republican	22	−2	1	−1	2	23
Democrat	4	−1	34	−2	1	37
American	13	0	−2	1	1	13
Not Eligible	3	0	0	0	5	8
Not Voting	1	5	−4	3	15	19
% Electorate 1860	42	3	28	2	25	

N = 63 counties

Table 8 / Ohio

Party in 1856	Party in 1860					
	Republican	Douglas Democrat	Breckinridge Democrat	Constitutional Union	Not Voting	% Electorate 1860
Republican	40	−2	2	0	−1	38
Democrat	0	38	1	−1	−4	35
American	3	−2	1	2	1	6
Not Eligible	2	3	−1	1	7	12
Not Voting	2	1	−1	0	7	10
% Electorate 1860	47	38	2	2	10	

N = 88 counties

Table 9 / Indiana

Party in 1856	Party in 1860					
	Republican	Douglas Democrat	Breckinridge Democrat	Constitutional Union	Not Voting	% Electorate 1860
Republican	30	−2	1	1	1	31
Democrat	0	35	3	−1	2	39
American	4	−3	2	2	2	7
Not Eligible	7	5	−2	0	2	12
Not Voting	4	4	−1	−1	4	10
% Electorate 1860	46	38	4	2	11	

N = 91 counties

Table 10 / Illinois

Party in 1856	Party in 1860					
	Republican	Douglas Democrat	Breckinridge Democrat	Constitutional Union	Not Voting	% Electorate 1860
Republican	24	−1	0	−1	3	25
Democrat	−4	29	2	1	−1	27
American	9	3	−1	0	−2	10
Not Eligible	13	6	0	0	1	21
Not Voting	2	3	0	0	12	18
% Electorate 1860·	44	41	1	1	13	

N = 99 counties

Table 11 / Iowa

Party in 1856	Party in 1860					
	Republican	Douglas Democrat	Breckinridge Democrat	Constitutional Union	Not Voting	% Electorate 1860
Republican	30	1	0	0	−1	30
Democrat	−1	24	0	0	2	26
American	5	1	0	1	−1	7
Not Eligible	11	9	0	0	11	31
Not Voting	2	2	0	0	3	7
% Electorate 1860	46	37	1	1	15	

N = 64 counties

TABLES 12–13 / ESTIMATED PROPORTIONS BETWEEN VOTING FOR
PRESIDENT 1856 AND GOVERNOR 1860

Table 12 / Indiana

Party in 1856	Party in 1860			
	Republican	Democrat	Not Voting	% Electorate 1860
Republican	30	0	1	31
Democrat	0	36	2	39
American	6	0	2	7
Not Eligible	6	3	3	12
Not Voting	3	2	5	10
% Electorate 1860	45	42	13	

N = 91 counties

Table 13 / Pennsylvania

	Party in 1860			
Party in 1856	Republican	Democrat	Not Voting	% Electorate 1860
Republican	20	−1	4	23
Democrat	5	34	−2	37
American	13	0	1	13
Not Eligible	2	1	5	8
Not Voting	1	3	15	19
% Electorate 1860	42	36	22	

N = 63 counties

Table 14 / Estimated Proportions between Voting for President 1856 and Supreme Court Justice 1860: Ohio

	Party in 1860			
Party in 1856	Republican	Democrat	Not Voting	% Electorate 1860
Republican	34	−2	7	38
Democrat	4	39	−9	35
American	3	1	2	6
Not Eligible	1	2	8	12
Not Voting	2	0	8	10
% Electorate 1860	43	41	16	

N = 88 counties

Table 15 / Party Percentages in Indiana and Illinois in 1856 and 1860

	1856			1860			
	Frémont	Buchanan	Fillmore	Lincoln	Douglas	Breckinridge	Bell
Indiana (State wide)	40.1	50.4	9.5	51.1	42.5	1.9	4.5
Southern counties	22.2	56.8	21.0	43.6	45.2	7.4	3.9
Illinois (State wide)	40.2	44.1	15.7	50.8	47.0	0.7	1.4
Southern counties	13.0	59.9	27.2	32.4	62.7	1.6	3.3

Table 16 / Estimated Percentages between Occupation and Voting for President

	Party in 1860	
	Republican	Democrat
MAINE		
Farmer	36%	16%
Manufacturing worker	38	35
N = 380 townships		
IOWA		
Farmer	45	45
Skilled worker	84	0
Unskilled laborer	28	37
N = 63 counties		
CINCINNATI		
Unskilled laborer	0	65
Skilled worker	56	29
N = 17 wards		
CHAUTAUQUA COUNTY		
Farmer	78	18
Worker and other	48	37
N = 25 townships		

Table 17 / Estimated Percentage of Germans Voting Republican in the
1856 and 1860 Presidential Elections

	Frémont	Lincoln	N
Iowa	3%	27%	63
New York	9	34	60
Ohio	46	43	41
Pennsylvania	3	44	18

N = counties

Table 18 / Estimated Percentage of Native Born Voting Republican
in the 1856 and 1860 Presidential Elections

| | Native Born | | |
	Frémont	Lincoln	N
Indiana	41%	49%	91
Iowa	45	50	63
New York	57	61	60
	Yankee		
Indiana	46	56	
Iowa	64	64	
New York	100	100	
	Southern		
Indiana	16	36	
Iowa	0	0	

N = counties

TABLES 19–23 / INFLUENCE OF EXPLANATORY VARIABLES ON REPUBLICAN
VOTE FOR PRESIDENT 1860

Table 19 / New York

Explanatory variables	Regression coefficient	Standard error	Beta coefficient	Change in R^2
Yankee	.94	.02	.34	.57
Born in Ireland	−.54	.02	−.37	.20
Black	−2.08	.07	−.23	.03
Presbyterian	.80	.02	.23	.01
Universalist	1.51	.09	.08	.01
Average farm value	−.00	.00	−.12	.01
Manufacturing capital/pop.	.01	.00	.14	.01

Mult. R = .92 R^2 = .85   N = 60 counties

Table 20 / Pennsylvania

Explanatory variables	Regression coefficient	Standard error	Beta coefficient	Change in R^2
Union Free Bethel	1.05	.03	.37	.15
Presbyterian	.20	.01	.33	.18
Yankee	.51	.01	.47	.14
Dutch Reform	−2.24	.06	−.25	.05
Born in Scotland	6.03	.19	.25	.02
Farms 10–100 acres	−.57	.02	−.39	.03
Quaker	.06	.02	.03	.02
Methodist	−.13	.01	−.14	.01
German Reform	.19	.01	.20	.01

Mult. R = .78 R^2 = .61   N = 63 counties

Table 21 / Ohio

Explanatory variables	Regression coefficient	Standard error	Beta coefficient	Change in R^2
Yankee	.23	.06	.14	.31
Born in Germany	−1.37	.06	−.65	.31
Quaker	.26	.01	.12	.03
Born in Ohio	−.75	.06	−.61	.02
Other foreign born	−2.76	.08	−.37	.02
German Reform	.61	.02	.19	.01
Lutheran	−.21	.01	−.13	.01
Southern born	−.96	.06	−.41	.01
Males 21–29	−.49	.03	−.10	.00
Congregational	−.26	.02	−.13	.01

Mult. R = .86 R^2 = .73   N = 88 counties

Table 22 / Indiana

Explanatory variables	Regression coefficient	Standard error	Beta coefficient	Change in R^2
Quaker	.42	.01	.24	.15
Yankee	.47	.04	.13	.20
Born in Germany	−.44	.02	−.25	.08
Born in Indiana	−.25	.01	−.23	.04
Born in England–Wales	−3.85	.22	−.22	.03
Per capita wealth	.01	.00	.17	.03
Southern born	−.47	.18	−.27	.02
Manufacturing capital/pop.	.00	.00	.14	.02
Improved acres	.13	.01	.12	.01
Presbyterian	−.16	.01	−.10	.01

Mult. R = .77 R^2 = .59   N = 89 counties

Table 23 / Illinois

Explanatory variables	Regression coefficient	Standard error	Beta coefficient	Change in R^2
Improved acres	.10	.01	.12	.62
Farms 10–100 acres	−.65	.02	−.22	.08
Yankee	−.18	.04	−.11	.08
Southern born	−.76	.04	−.43	.02
Catholic	−.18	.01	−.09	.01
Born in Illinois	−.75	.04	−.43	.01
Males 50 and above	1.34	.04	.23	.01
German Reform	−2.40	.09	−.10	.01
Presbyterian	.13	.01	.06	.01
Born in England–Wales	1.29	.07	.12	.01
Males 21–29	.71	.04	.17	.01

Mult. R = .92 R^2 = .85   N = 95 counties

Explanatory variables	Regression coefficient	Standard error	Beta coefficient
ILLINOIS			
Baptist	.02	.01	.01
Congregational	.21	.02	.06
German Reform	−2.40	.09	−.10
Lutheran	−.38	.03	−.07
Methodist	−.05	.01	−.03
Presbyterian	.13	.01	.06
Quaker	.65	.06	.04
Catholic	−.18	.01	−.09
INDIANA			
Baptist	−.06	.01	−.08
Congregational	−.07★	.06	−.01
Episcopal	−.35	.08	−.05
German Reform	−1.58	.09	−.12
Lutheran	−.17	.02	−.06
Methodist	−.01★	.01	−.01
Presbyterian	−.16	.01	−.10
Quaker	.42	.01	.24
Catholic	−.09	.01	−.05
NEW YORK			
Baptist	−.06	.02	−.01
Congregational	.30	.03	.04
Dutch Reform	.01	.02★	.00
Episcopal	−1.50	.05	−.21
German Reform	7.49	.32	.15
Lutheran	−.45	.03	−.06
Methodist	−.95	.03	−.24
Presbyterian	.50	.02	.15
Quaker	1.72	.12	.07
Catholic	−.78	.03	−.39
OHIO			
Baptist	.17	.01	.12
Congregational	−.26	.02	−.13
Episcopal	−.18	.03	−.03
German Reform	.61	.02	.19
Lutheran	−.21	.01	−.13

Table 24 (continued)

Explanatory variables	Regression coefficient	Standard error	Beta coefficient
OHIO (continued)			
Methodist	−.01	.00	−.02
Presbyterian	−.06	.01	−.06
Quaker	.26	.01	.12
Catholic	−.14	.01	−.10
PENNSYLVANIA			
Baptist	.01*	.01	.01
Episcopal	−.19	.04	−.05
German Reform	.19	.01	.20
Methodist	−.13	.01	−.14
Presbyterian	.20	.01	.33
Quaker	.06	.02	.03
Catholic	.04	.01	.03

*Not significant at .05 level

Table 25 / Influence of Per Capita Wealth on Republican Vote for President 1860

	Regression coefficient	Standard error	Beta coefficient
Illinois	.015	.001	.16
Indiana	.013	.001	.17
New York	.009	.000	.14
Ohio	.002	.001	.03
Pennsylvania	.005	.001	.09

NOTES

Research for this essay was funded in part by grants from the University of Wyoming's Office of the Vice President for Research and the Henry E. Huntington Library, and necessary computer time was made available by the University of Wyoming. Some of the election returns and census data utilized in this study were provided by the Interuniversity Consortium for Political and Social Research, Ann Arbor. The 1860 census sample for Cincinnati was done by Carl Abbott and made available through the Consortium (ICPSR Study Number 7456). Paul Goodman generously allowed me to use the election returns and census data he compiled for Maine and Massachusetts, which supplemented my own files for these states. I also wish to thank George B. Forgie and Mark E. Neely, Jr., who read a draft of this essay, for a number of helpful comments and suggestions. Of course, neither the Consortium nor these individuals bear any responsibility for the interpretations presented in this essay.

1 / *The Diary of George Templeton Strong,* ed. Allan Nevins and Milton Halsey Thomas, 4 vols. (New York: Macmillan, 1952), 3:59; *The Diary of Calvin Fletcher,* ed. Gayle Thornbrough, Dorothy L. Riker, and Paula Corpuz, 9 vols. (Indianapolis: Indiana Historical Society, 1972–83), 6:625; *New York World,* November 7, 1860. Hereafter unless otherwise indicated, the year for newspaper and manuscript citations is 1860.

2 / *New York Weekly Tribune,* November 10, 17; *Missouri Democrat,* November 7, 8; *Illinois State Journal,* November 8; John G. Nicolay, Memo, November 6, John G. Nicolay Papers, Library of Congress; Mercie A. Conkling to Clinton L. Conkling, November 6, James C. and Clinton L. Conkling Papers, Illinois State Historical Library.

3 / The fullest study of the 1860 election is Reinhard Luthin, *The First Lincoln Campaign* (Cambridge: Harvard University Press, 1944) which supersedes Emerson D. Fite, *The Presidential Campaign of 1860* (New York: Macmillan, 1911). Shorter treatments include: James Ford Rhodes, *History of the United States from the Compromise of 1850,* 7 vols. (New York: Macmillan, 1892–1906), 2:396–458; William E. Baringer, *Lincoln's Rise to Power* (Boston: Little, Brown and Co., 1937), 296–329; Allan Nevins, *The Emergence of Lincoln,* 2 vols. (New York: Charles Scribner's Sons, 1950), 2:261–317; Glyndon G. Van Deusen, "Why the Republican Party Came to Power," in *The Crisis of the Union, 1860–1861,* ed. George Harmon Knoles (Baton Rouge: LSU, 1965), 3–20; Don E. Fehrenbacher, "The Election of 1860," in *Crucial American Elections* (Philadelphia: American Philosophical Society, 1973), 30–41; and David M. Potter, *The Impending Crisis, 1848–1861,* ed. and completed by Don E. Fehrenbacher (New York: Harper and Row, 1976), 405–47.

4 / William E. Baringer, "The Republican Triumph," in *Politics and the Crisis of 1860,* ed. Norman A. Graebner (Urbana: University of Illinois Press, 1961), 92; Nevins, *Emergence of Lincoln,* 2:313.

5 / Ollinger Crenshaw, "Urban and Rural Voting in the Election of 1860," in *Historiography and Urbanization: Essays in American History in Honor of W. Stull Holt,* ed. Eric F. Goldman (Baltimore: The Johns Hopkins University Press, 1941), 43–66, is a pioneering work on voting patterns in 1860. Other studies include: Michael F. Holt, *Forging a Majority: The Formation of the Republican Party in Pittsburgh, 1848–1860* (New Haven: Yale University Press, 1969); Stephen L. Hansen, *The Making of the Third Party System: Voters and Parties in Illinois, 1850–1876* (Ann Arbor: UMI Research Press, Inc., 1980); Dale Baum, *The Civil War Party System: The Case of Massachusetts, 1848–1876* (Chapel Hill: University of North Carolina Press, 1984); and Thomas W. Kremm, "Cleveland and the First Lincoln Election: The Ethnic Response to Nativism," *Journal of Interdisciplinary History* 8 (1977): 69–86. One exception is the political allegiance of Germans in 1860, which has been extensively studied.

6 / Horace Greeley, *The American Conflict,* 2 vols. (Hartford, Conn.: C. D. Case and Co., 1866), 1:299–300.

7 / Reinhard H. Luthin, "Organizing the Republican Party in the 'Border-Slave' Regions: Edward Bates's Presidential Candidacy in 1860," *Missouri Historical Review* 38 (1944): 138–61.

8 / Republicans narrowly carried the Connecticut gubernatorial election by only 600 votes out of over 90,000 cast, while in Rhode Island, Americans formed a coalition with the Democrats after the Republicans nominated a staunch antislavery man to head their

state ticket, with the result that the Republican party lost the governorship it previously held. James L. Huston, "The Threat of Radicalism: Seward's Candidacy and the Rhode Island Gubernatorial Election of 1860," *Rhode Island History* 41 (1982): 87–99.

9 / FitzHenry Warren to James Shepherd Pike, February 2, in Pike, *First Blows of the Civil War* (New York: American News Co., 1879), 483. Also see Henry C. Carey to Thomas H. Dudley, November 25, 1859, John L. N. Stratton to Dudley, April 4, Russell Errett to Dear Sir, April 17, *Private,* lithographed letter, Thomas H. Dudley Papers, Henry E. Huntington Library; John L. Wilson to William H. Seward, April 1, John L. Wilson Papers, Illinois State Historical Library; George D. Morgan to Edwin D. Morgan, April 3, Edwin D. Morgan Papers, New York State Library.

10 / Because of Lincoln's nomination, the Chicago convention has been extensively covered in the historical literature. See in particular Baringer, *Lincoln's Rise to Power,* 188–295; Luthin, *First Lincoln Campaign,* 136–67; Nevins, *Emergence of Lincoln,* 2:229–60; Don E. Fehrenbacher, "The Republican Decision at Chicago," in Graebner, *Politics and the Crisis of 1860,* 32–60; and Kenneth M. Stampp, "The Republican National Convention of 1860," *The Imperiled Union: Essays on the Background of the Civil War* (New York: Oxford University Press, 1980), 136–62. Two important sources are C. W. Johnson, comp., *Proceedings of the First Three Republican National Conventions* (Minneapolis: Harrison and Smith, 1893); and William B. Hesseltine, ed., *Three against Lincoln: Murat Halstead Reports the Caucuses of 1860* (Baton Rouge: LSU, 1960), 141–77.

11 / Greeley to Mrs. R. M. Whipple, [April], quoted in Jeter Isely, *Horace Greeley and the Republican Party, 1853–1861* (Princeton: Princeton University Press, 1947), 266.

12 / Isaac Hill Bromley, "What Caused the Defeat of Mr. Seward," in *Intimate Memories of Lincoln,* ed. Rufus Rockwell Wilson (Elmira, N.Y.: Primavera Press, 1945), 284.

13 / Don E. Fehrenbacher, *Prelude to Greatness: Lincoln in the 1850's* (Stanford: Stanford University Press, 1962), 156–57 n; Eric Foner, *Free Soil, Free Labor, Free Men: The Ideology of the Republican Party before the Civil War* (New York: Oxford University Press, 1970), 132–33; and Richard H. Sewell, *Ballots for Freedom: Antislavery Politics in the United States, 1837–1860* (New York: Oxford University Press, 1976), 362–63, deny that the 1860 platform represented a conservative retreat from the doctrines endorsed in 1856. Like all political platforms, that of the Republicans in 1860 contained a certain amount of ambiguity, and these historians' points are a useful corrective, but nevertheless I think, on the whole, the platform was more moderate and more general than that of 1856.

14 / Historians have tended to exaggerate the extent to which the Republican party adopted protectionism as a party principle before the Civil War. Party members who supported free trade insisted afterwards without straining its language that the platform called for nothing more than "the establishment of a revenue tariff bill with incidental protection" (*The Memoirs of Gustave Koerner, 1809–1896,* ed. Thomas J. McCormack, 2 vols. [Cedar Rapids, Iowa: Torch Press, 1909], 2:187).

15 / Bromley, "Defeat of Seward," 284.

16 / Joseph Casey to Leonard Swett, May 26, David Davis Family Papers, Illinois State Historical Library; Elihu B. Washburne to Abraham Lincoln, May 20, James E. Harvey to Lincoln, May 21, *Private,* L. K. Pangborn to Josiah M. Lucas, May 22, enclosed in Lucas to Lincoln, May 24, Nehemiah D. Sperry to Lincoln, May 27, Abraham Lincoln Papers, Library of Congress. Whether in response to this advice or more likely out of an understanding of the wisdom of caution, Lincoln's letter of acceptance was phrased in general terms and made no direct reference to any platform plank. *The Collected Works of Abraham Lincoln,* ed. Roy P. Basler, Marion Delores Pratt, and Lloyd A. Dunlap, 9 vols. (New Brunswick, N.J.: Rutgers University Press, 1953–55), 4:52.

17 / Baringer, *Lincoln's Rise to Power*, 195; *Chicago Press and Tribune*, May 16. Also see Israel D. Andrews to Nathaniel P. Banks, Jr., July 8, 1859, Nathaniel P. Banks, Jr., Papers, Illinois State Historical Library; Richard M. Corwine to Lincoln, May 28, Lincoln Papers; James E. Harvey to Simon Cameron, June 29, Simon Cameron Papers, Historical Society of Dauphin County; Norman Eastman to William H. Seward, July 5, William H. Seward Papers, University of Rochester; R. Hosea to Salmon P. Chase, May 18, Salmon P. Chase Papers, Library of Congress; James G. Blaine, *Twenty Years in Congress*, 2 vols. (Norwich, Conn.: Henry Bill Publishing Co., 1884–86), 1:165–66.

18 / Francis P. Blair, Jr., to William Dennison, n.d. [late May?], Illinois State Historical Library.

19 / Blaine, *Twenty Years of Congress*, 1:165. For examples of Republican confidence, see James E. Harvey to Cameron, June 26, 29, Cameron Papers, HSDC; William M. Evarts to Edwards Pierrepont, July 18, Edwards Pierrepont Papers, Yale University.

20 / For these aspects of the party's ideology, see Foner, *Free Soil, Free Labor, Free Men;* and William E. Gienapp, "The Republican Party and the Slave Power," in *New Perspectives on Race and Slavery in America,* ed. Robert H. Abzug and Stephen E. Maizlish (Lexington: University Press of Kentucky, 1986).

21 / Reuben Vose, *The Life and Speeches of Abraham Lincoln and Hannibal Hamlin,* quoted in James G. Randall, *Lincoln the President,* 4 vols. (New York: Dodd, Meade and Co., 1945–55), 1:187.

22 / Edward L. Pierce to Charles H. Ray, August 9, Charles H. Ray Papers, Henry E. Huntington Library; *Philadelphia North American* quoted in Osborn H. Oldroyd, *Lincoln's Campaign, or the Political Revolution of 1860* (Chicago: Laird and Lee, 1896), 126.

23 / Oglesby's connection with the railsplitter story is documented in his papers for 1860 (Richard J. Oglesby Papers, Illinois State Historical Library). Also see John Hanks's testimony, *Illinois State Journal,* July 16; James T. Hickey, "Oglesby's Fence Rail Dealings and the 1860 Decatur Convention," *Journal of the Illinois State Historical Society* 54 (1961): 5–24.

24 / Luthin, *First Lincoln Campaign,* 169.

25 / For Lincoln's reputation for honesty and its effect on the 1860 campaign, see Gabor S. Boritt, "Was Lincoln a Vulnerable Candidate in 1860?" *Civil War History* 27 (1981): 32–48. The nickname Abe, which was almost universally invoked by Republican propaganda to strengthen his image as one of the people, was strictly for partisan purposes. Lincoln hated it and never used it. Buchanan's record is discussed in David E. Meerse, "Buchanan, Corruption and the Election of 1860," *Civil War History* 12 (1966): 116–31.

26 / *Lincoln Weekly Herald,* October 5, Research Files, Abraham Lincoln Association Papers, Illinois State Historical Library. Also see William M. Green to Oglesby, June 15, Oglesby Papers.

27 / Cf. H. Preston James, "Political Pageantry in the Campaign of 1860 in Illinois," *Abraham Lincoln Quarterly* 4 (1947): 313–47.

28 / For a history of the Wide-Awakes, see the *New York Herald,* September 19.

29 / While a majority of members were doubtless eligible to vote, clubs generally accepted younger members. The Wide Awake Club in Waterbury, Connecticut, for example, set the minimum age for initiates at eighteen years. Waterbury Wide Awake Club Record Book, Connecticut Historical Society.

30 / *Chicago Democrat,* September 24; William H. Brandenburg to Thurlow Weed, October 1, Thurlow Weed Papers, University of Rochester. Another New Yorker indicated that the members of a local Wide Awake club "are to a great extent young men

. . . and at least half of them have never voted a Republican Ticket" (James W. Husted to Morgan, August 1, Morgan Papers).

31 / Michael F. Holt makes this point in *The Political Crisis of the 1850s* (New York: John Wiley and Sons, 1979), 176. One Democratic editor even dismissed the Wide-Awakes as a group of Know-Nothings. *Illinois State Register,* August 1. For evidence that the Wide-Awakes drew from young, less affluent workingmen and farmers (probably mostly sons and hired hands), see James Irving Smith to Morgan, October 8; James W. Husted to Morgan, August 1, Morgan Papers; records of the Wide Awake Club, Paris, Illinois, Asa J. Baber Papers, Illinois State Historical Library.

32 / The tortuous negotiations to form a fusion electoral ticket in New York are detailed in the Samuel L. M. Barlow Papers, Henry E. Huntington Library.

33 / Historians such as James G. Randall who emphasize the impact of the electoral college on the result ignore the more basic point that a sectional party—at least one that took as its goal national power—was not feasible except with some system such as the electoral college which under certain circumstances awarded a candidate with a minority of the popular vote a majority of presidential electors. Republican organizers had taken this factor into account from the party's founding, since no party in the antebellum period realistically could hope to win a majority of the popular vote without significant support in at least some parts of the South. To taunts about being a sectional organization, Republicans rejoined that if allowed to contest elections in the slave states without interference, they would soon develop a southern constituency. Historians who lament the undemocratic features of the electoral college usually silently pass over the use of intimidation and coercion to prevent the Republican party from running candidates in the South, surely a more direct denial of the basic principles of the American political system. Randall, *Lincoln,* 1:194, 200–201. For a fascinating discussion of how alternative state boundaries proposed by Thomas Jefferson might have altered the outcome of the election, see Thomas B. Alexander, "The Civil War as Institutional Fulfillment," *Journal of Southern History* 47 (1981): 22–28. Alexander's article is the best analysis of the role of the electoral college in the election.

34 / William E. Gienapp, " 'Politics Seem to Enter into Everything': Political Culture in the North, 1840–1860," in *Essays on American Antebellum Politics, 1840–1860,* ed. Stephen E. Maizlish and John J. Kushma (College Station: Texas A&M University Press, 1982), 17–20.

35 / This study is based on the analysis of voting patterns in nine northern states: Maine, Massachusetts, and Connecticut in New England, New York and Pennsylvania of the middle states, Ohio, Indiana, and Illinois from the Old Northwest, and Iowa in the Trans-Mississippi West. This sample includes the most populous and influential northern states, as well as the most important doubtful states. The voting analysis utilizes the statistical technique of ecological regression to derive estimates of the transition in voting from one election to another. Since this procedure is based on assumptions that are not always entirely satisfied in reality, these figures should be considered estimates rather than precise proportions. Negative estimates can be interpreted as essentially zero; such results are not unusual when a group overwhelmingly votes in one direction. The regressions are weighted by the number of voters in each county or township in 1860 (this procedure alters somewhat the 1856 marginals from each party's actual percentage). The number of cases is given by N. The not-eligible category refers to voters enfranchised between the two elections being compared (young men who attained adulthood and immigrants who were naturalized). Nonvoters were eligible to vote in the earlier election but for whatever reason did not participate. Subject to the errors of rounding, the proportions added across

or down equal the marginals. The rows of the tables indicate how the supporters of a party divided in a subsequent election (in table 3, for example, 34/40 or approximately 85 percent of Frémont's supporters in Maine voted for Lincoln). The columns give the proportion each group contributed to a party's vote (again in table 3, Frémont men represented 34/38 or about 89 percent of Lincoln's vote in the state). Party percentages are of the total electorate rather than the total vote. The method of calculating the number of eligible voters in these states is detailed in the appendix of my essay, " 'Politics Seem to Enter into Everything.' " For a discussion of the technique of ecological regression and its limitations, see J. Morgan Kousser, "Ecological Regression and the Analysis of Past Politics," *Journal of Interdisciplinary History* 4 (1974): 1–14; W. Phillips Shively, " 'Ecological' Inference: The Use of Aggregate Data to Study Individuals," *American Political Science Review* 63 (1969): 1183–96; Donald E. Stokes, "Cross-Level Inference as a Game Against Nature," in *Mathematical Applications in Political Science,* ed. Joseph L. Bernd (Charlottesville: University of Virginia Press, 1969), 4:62–83; and Laura Irwin Langbein and Allan J. Lichtman, *Ecological Inference* (Beverly Hills, Calif.: Sage Publications, 1978).

36 / R. C. Slaughter to his brother, March 2, 1861, Miscellaneous Collections, Filson Club; *Buffalo Commercial Advertiser,* quoted in Luthin, *First Lincoln Campaign,* 211. Austin Baldwin to John A. Rockwell, July 2, John A. Rockwell Papers, Henry E. Huntington Library. I wish to thank Daniel W. Crofts for a copy of the first letter cited.

37 / For assertions to this effect, see Samuel L. M. Barlow to John Slidell, November 27, Copy, Barlow Papers; August Belmont to John Forsyth, November 22, *Letters, Speeches, and Addresses of August Belmont* (n.p., 1890), 24; *New York Herald,* November 26; Samuel J. Tilden quoted in Luthin, *First Lincoln Campaign,* 218. Historians who have adopted this line of argument include Luthin, 221–23, 226–27; and Nevins, *Emergence of Lincoln,* 2:312.

38 / William P. Forman to Seward, November 6, Seward Papers; M. W. Stevens to John P. Hale, October 30, John P. Hale Papers, New Hampshire Historical Society.

39 / Alexander K. McClure to Lincoln, October 15, Lincoln Papers. McClure apparently erred, however, in predicting that "many" Douglas men "will not vote at all."

40 / Republicans conceded that only the Democratic split gave them any chance in Oregon and California. Cornelius C. Cole to Morgan, February 23, William H. Walkins to Morgan, [summer], Morgan Papers; Lincoln to Anson G. Henry, September 22, *Collected Works of Lincoln,* 4:118.

41 / The totals in the state contests were: Indiana (governor), Lane (Republican), 136,275 (51.9 percent); Hendricks (Democrat), 126,968 (48.1 percent); Ohio (Supreme Court justice), Brinkerhoff (Republican), 212,854 (51.6 percent); Smith (Democrat), 199,951 (48.4 percent); and Pennsylvania (governor), Curtin (People's), 262,403 (53.3 percent); Foster (Democrat), 230,239 (46.7 percent).

42 / The Democratic total declined by about 35,000 votes in the presidential contest, but scrutiny of tables 7 and 13 suggests that the bulk of this dropoff came from recent recruits (new voters and previous nonvoters) rather than from longtime party supporters.

43 / Both the Democrats' and Republicans' strength among new voters and previous nonvoters increased in Indiana and declined in Ohio in the presidential election. In Pennsylvania, the Republicans scored a modest gain among these voters while the Democratic proportion fell sharply. Most of these defectors apparently backed Bell rather than Lincoln, since the proportion of new voters and earlier nonvoters who abstained was the same in the state and national contests. Probably most were not regular Democrats but conservatives who cast Democratic ballots in the state election only because there was no Constitutional Union ticket.

44 / Herndon quoted in Luthin, *First Lincoln Campaign,* 184; James E. Harvey to Lincoln, July 27, Lincoln Papers. Also see the *New York Tribune,* July 17, 28; Dan Bush to Ozias M. Hatch, May 24, Ozias M. Hatch Papers, Illinois State Historical Library; *New York Herald,* November 26.

45 / Former Americans were essential to the Republican margin of victory in Illinois and Pennsylvania. Lincoln would have carried New York and Indiana if his American supporters had sat out the election or, in the latter state, thrown their votes away on Bell, but not if they had voted for the fusion ticket in New York (which was quite likely) and the Douglas electors in Indiana. This situation also prevailed in Iowa.

46 / Edward J. C. Atterbury to Rockwell, September 7, S. H. White to Rockwell, July 1, Rockwell Papers.

47 / R. C. Slaughter to his brother, March 2, 1861, Miscellaneous Collections, Filson Club; *Buffalo Commercial Advertiser,* quoted in Luthin, *First Lincoln Campaign,* 211; *New York Tribune,* July 17.

48 / See the discussion of this question in Potter, *Impending Crisis,* 429–30.

49 / James E. Harvey to Cameron, June 29, Cameron Papers, HSDC. Sewardites naturally insisted that the Republicans could have won with their favorite at the head of the ticket. Caleb S. Henry to Frances A. Seward, September 19, John M. Bradford to William H. Seward, July 2, Seward Papers.

50 / For conjectures on this point, see the *New York Tribune,* July 16, October 4.

51 / Crenshaw, "Urban and Rural Voting in 1860."

52 / Quoted in Foner, *Free Soil, Free Labor, Free Men,* 306 n.

53 / David K. Wells Kilbourne to William Leighton, October 27, Hiram Barney Papers, Henry E. Huntington Library; John Dunham to Rockwell, August 30, Rockwell Papers; George D. Morgan to Edwin D. Morgan, October 22, Morgan Papers; Thurlow Weed to Lincoln, August 13, David Davis to Lincoln, August 18, George G. Fogg to Lincoln, September 14, Lincoln Papers; *New York Tribune,* November 7. John Z. Goodrich, one of the party's chief fundraisers, said of the situation in Boston: "The monied & commercial men there are in the Bell [and] Everett movement" (Goodrich to Cameron, October 24, Simon Cameron Papers, Library of Congress). Cf. Philip S. Foner, *Business and Slavery: The New York Merchants and the Irrepressible Conflict* (Chapel Hill: University of North Carolina Press, 1941).

54 / *Intimate Letters of Carl Schurz, 1841–1869,* ed. Joseph Schafer (Madison: State Historical Society of Wisconsin, 1928), 180. See the evidence below concerning the influence of nativity and wealth on party loyalty.

55 / Foner, *Free Soil, Free Labor, Free Men,* 35. Schurz, for example, in the letter cited in the previous note declared that the Republican party was composed "chiefly of . . . the native American farmers."

56 / *Springfield Republican,* November 1, 1856.

57 / Stephen Miller to Cameron, April 2, Cameron Papers, LC; Lovejoy quoted in Luthin, *First Lincoln Campaign,* 186.

58 / Nevins, *Emergence of Lincoln,* 2:302. Van Deusen, "Why the Republican Party Came to Power," in Knoles, *Crisis of the Union,* 6, 12, and Luthin, *First Lincoln Campaign,* 177–78, present a similar argument. Don Fehrenbacher effectively questions the issue's significance in his comment on Van Deusen's article, "Comment on Why the Republican Party Came to Power," in Knoles, *Crisis of the Union,* 26–27.

59 / Blaine, *Twenty Years of Congress,* 1:207; Cameron quoted in Luthin, *First Lincoln Campaign,* 208. Endorsing these assertions, James Ford Rhodes declared without qualification that "the prominence given the tariff question . . . contributed more than any

other one factor to the result in Pennsylvania" (*History of the United States*, 2:454–55). Both Holt, *Forging a Majority*, 278–79, 310, and Fehrenbacher, "Comment on Why the Republicans Came to Power," 28–29, question the importance of the tariff issue in Pennsylvania voting.

60 / Luthin, *First Lincoln Campaign*, 208; *Philadelphia North American* quoted in Randall, *Lincoln the President*, 1:189. Luthin notes that the *North American* ran many more editorials on the tariff than on slavery during the campaign.

61 / In a multiple regression analysis, the proportion of iron workers, while positively related to the Republican vote, was the weakest of all explanatory variables and did not increase the proportion of explained variance by even .001 percent (the regression coefficient is .006, which is not significant at the .05 level, and the beta coefficient is .001). Furthermore, the proportion of coal and iron workers combined had no influence on Lincoln's vote. If one includes the proportion of the population born in England-Wales rather than Ireland in the equation, the signs of the regression coefficient for iron workers, and for iron workers and coal miners combined, are both negative. Multicollinearity prevents inclusion of both those born in Ireland and in England-Wales in the same equation, but since many of the iron workers and coal miners in the state were English and Welsh, the latter result is probably more accurate. Once ethnicity is controlled for, in other words, the weak relationship between iron workers and Lincoln's vote disappears. For an explanation of multiple regression, see note 63.

62 / Republican leaders, of course, did not know the results in advance and hence devoted considerable attention to Pennsylvania in order to make Lincoln's election certain. Assertions about the crucial importance of the tariff issue are normally based on the incorrect assumption that Lincoln had to carry the Keystone State to win.

63 / Tables 19–25 are based on the statistical technique of multiple regression, which seeks to determine the relationship between a dependent variable (in this case, the Republican vote in 1860) and an independent variable (wealth, religion, ethnicity, and so forth) when the influence of the other independent variables is controlled. The sign indicates the direction of the relationship (a positive sign means that as the independent variable increases in strength, so does the dependent variable), and the regression coefficient indicates the strength of the relationship. In this analysis, the relationship is linear. Most variables are percentages of the population. Except for New York, religion is measured by church seats as a ratio of the population, and the figures on ethnicity have been extrapolated from the 1870 census, adjusted by the proportions of native and foreign born for each county given in the 1860 census. For New York, the statistics on church attendance and place of birth in the 1855 state census have been used instead. Since variables are measured in different units (church seats, dollars, percentages of the population, etc.) the standardized beta coefficients allow one to compare the relative influence of variables on the Republican vote (a variable with a beta coefficient twice as great as that for another variable has twice the influence on the Republican vote when the effects of the other independent variables are controlled). Beta coefficients unfortunately are not unaffected by the process of aggregation, but they are necessary when, as in this study, variables are measured in different units. In table 19, the regression coefficient indicates that an increase of 1 percent in the Yankee population (when the other variables are controlled) increases Lincoln's vote by .94 percent; at the same time, an identical increase in the Irish population reduces (since the sign of the coefficient is negative) Lincoln's vote by .54 percent. Since both of these variables are measured in the same units (percentage of the population) the regression coefficients can be compared directly. However, average farm value cannot be easily compared with these variables because it is measured in different units (dol-

lars per farm). The beta coefficient allows such a comparison. It indicates that while both the Irish population and farm value are negatively related to Lincoln's vote when the other variables are held constant, an increase of one standard deviation unit in the Irish population has three times the effect on Lincoln's vote as the same change in the average farm value (−.37 versus −.12). The regression equations are weighted by the square root of the population in 1860. With only a couple of noted exceptions, the regression coefficients are significant at the .05 level or better, or in other words, the probability is .95 or better that the true coefficient is not 0 (which would mean that there was no relationship between the variables). The number of cases (counties) is given by N. The multiple R indicates the strength of the linear relationship between the set of independent variables and the dependent variable, and R^2 indicates the proportion of total variance explained by the equation. If two of the independent variables are very strongly related, regression analysis cannot always calculate reliable coefficients; therefore, to guard against this problem, which is known as multicollinearity, if two independent variables had a correlation of .75 or greater, one was dropped from the analysis. In tables 19–23, variables that contributed less than 1 percent of the explained variance have been omitted. For a discussion of multiple regression, see Hubert M. Blalock, Jr., *Social Statistics,* 2d ed. rev. (New York: McGraw-Hill, 1979), 451–508; Michael S. Lewis-Beck, *Applied Regression: An Introduction* (Beverly Hills, Calif.: Sage Publications, 1980); and Allan J. Lichtman, "Correlations, Regression, and the Ecological Fallacy: A Critique," *Journal of Interdisciplinary History* 4 (1974): 417–33, which is especially sensitive to the problems presented by data commonly used by historians.

64 / Baum finds wealth to be a more important influence on voting in Massachusetts (*Civil War Party System,* 85–89). High multicollinearity among many of the wealth variables and some ethnicity variables precludes employing Baum's exact methodology in this study.

65 / *New York Herald,* December 9; *Illinois State Journal,* November 10.

66 / Frederick C. Luebke, ed., *Ethnic Voters and the Election of Lincoln* (Lincoln: University of Nebraska Press, 1971), conveniently collects much of this literature.

67 / Based on the statistics for heads of households given in Mark Hornberger, "The Spatial Distribution of Ethnic Groups in Selected Counties in Pennsylvania: A Geographic Interpretation" (Ph.D. diss., Pennsylvania State University, 1974). Hornberger's figures combine immigrants and their native-born descendants, many of whom, such as the Pennsylvania Dutch, maintained attributes of their European cultural heritage. The small number of cases produces greater uncertainty in the regression estimates, though they probably accurately indicate the direction each group voted.

68 / *Memoirs of Koerner,* 2:21.

69 / Joshua Wagonselles [?] to Lyman Trumbull, November 12, Lyman Trumbull Papers, Library of Congress; *Illinois State Journal,* November 10. The available data does not allow for a precise analysis of German voting by age cohorts.

70 / For evidence on the behavior of Scandinavian, Dutch, and British voters, see the articles by George H. Daniels, Robert P. Swierenga, and Ronald P. Formisano, in Luebke, *Ethnic Voters and the Election of Lincoln.*

71 / *Illinois State Journal,* November 12. For Republican attacks on southern values and culture, see Foner, *Free Soil, Free Labor, Free Men,* 40–72.

72 / These estimates are derived from ecological regressions using place of birth for Indiana in 1850 and Iowa in 1856. The Iowa data are from the state census of 1856, and that for Indiana from the laborious compilations of Joseph E. Layton, "Sources of Population in Indiana, 1816–1850," *Bulletin of the Indiana State Library* 11 (1916): 2–26.

73 / The most extensive statement of this view is Paul Kleppner, *The Third Electoral System, 1853–1892: Parties, Voters, and Political Cultures* (Chapel Hill: University of North Carolina Press, 1979). Baum, *Civil War Party System*, 78–100, challenges this interpretation for Massachusetts voting.

74 / Because southern migrants to the midwestern states were members of the same evangelical churches—Baptists, Methodists, and Presbyterians—it is important to control for place of birth in order to assess the impact of religion on voting. In general, ethnicity seems to have been more crucial than religion in determining voting preference, though both exerted considerable influence and generally were more important than wealth. Moreover, voting among ethnic groups, while more consistent than religion, also displayed significant variations from one state to another.

75 / F. Reed to Hale, November 5, Hale Papers.

76 / Seward quoted in Rhodes, *History of the United States*, 2:441; John Z. Goodrich to Cameron, September 26, Cameron Papers, LC. Also see Lewis Benedict to Morgan, September 11, Morgan Papers. Bell leaders, on the other hand, noted that their movement was crippled by the absence of active young men to push the cause. Osmyn Baker to Rockwell, September 26, Rockwell Papers.

77 / See the discussion of this point in my essay, " 'Politics Seem to Enter into Everything,' " 53–61.

S T E P H E N   B .   O A T E S

*

Abraham Lincoln: Republican in the White House

THERE IS A POPULAR ARGUMENT IN THE ACADEMIES THAT Abraham Lincoln was "a Whig in the White House" who adhered to some theoretical Whig formula about a restricted presidency beyond what was necessary to save the Union. David Donald, a distinguished Civil War historian and biographer, introduced the "Whig-in-the-White-House" argument in an essay collected in the second edition of his *Lincoln Reconsidered.*[1] There Donald contended that the Lincoln presidency posed "a peculiar paradox." On the one hand, Lincoln was a strong president who expanded and enlarged executive power in unprecedented acts: he entrusted federal funds to private individuals for the public defense, summoned the militia to suppress a giant domestic insurrection, increased the size of the regular army, laid down rules of military conduct, authorized military law in vast areas behind Union lines, sanctioned the arrest of civilians on a scale undreamed of in America, issued an Emancipation Proclamation, and set about building loyal state regimes in conquered Dixie—all without consulting Congress. On the other hand, Donald notes, Lincoln was simultaneously a weak chief executive who abdicated his powers, bowing "not only to the will but to the caprice of the legislators." He seldom initiated legislation on Capitol Hill and used the veto less than any other important American

98

president. Beyond signing his name, he had little connection with the homestead, tariff, railroad, and banking bills that flowed out of the wartime Capitol and altered the role of government in the national economy. What was more, Donald contends, Lincoln had almost no influence on diplomacy and exercised scant control over his own executive departments.

How to account for the passive side of Lincoln's presidency? Here is how Donald's explanation might be summarized. It is not, as many scholars have argued, that Lincoln was too busy with the war to propose legislation or run his cabinet. After all, he found time to deal with an extraordinary amount of minutiae. Nor is it because he was temperamentally unsuited to administration. The explanation, Donald hypothesizes, is that Lincoln had a Whig view of his office: that is, he believed that the president should confine himself largely to executive functions and leave legislation to Congress.

Lincoln supposedly had held this view since his schooling as a Whig legislator and congressman in the 1830s and 1840s. Hating what they regarded as Andrew Jackson's executive usurpations, Whigs of that time advocated a weak president who might advise but would never dictate to Congress. According to Donald, Congressman Lincoln also opposed a strong chief executive—witness his flaying of President James K. Polk for vetoing river and harbor improvements. When the Whig party disintegrated in the 1850s, Lincoln disliked the idea of being "un-Whigged," Donald writes, and was "rather reluctant" to leave his cherished old party for another affiliation. Right here is the crux of Donald's argument. Lincoln grudgingly joined the Republicans, but took with him the Whig creed of a narrowly circumscribed chief executive. And he retained that creed when he became president, which was why he refused to introduce legislation on almost all issues except that of slavery. As Donald sees it, Lincoln's reluctance to control his cabinet was rooted in Whig doctrine, too, which opposed executive tyranny over departmental subordinates.

Yet Lincoln found himself in an unprecedented war in which Whig dogma could not always guide him. Thus, when necessity demanded, as it did in the matter of emancipation, Lincoln flexed his executive muscles and exercised the war power quite as though Congress did not exist. "Necessity," said Lincoln, "knows no law." Yet, Donald maintains, this also was sound Whig doctrine, because the old party bigwigs had defended a vigorous executive use of the war power. Thus, in weakly deferring to Congress and yet strongly asserting his war power when necessity compelled him, Lincoln was following the Whig creed in which he had been schooled. Here, then, is the explanation for "the puzzling ambiguity of his presidency," Donald writes. Paraphrasing one of Lincoln's own memorable statements, Donald concludes that the Civil War president could never "disenthrall" himself from his own Whig education.

Beguiling in its clarity and precision, Donald's essay seduced an entire generation of Civil War and Lincoln scholars. In his own seminal work, *The Era of Reconstruction* (1965), Kenneth M. Stampp argued that Lincoln remained to his dying day a practical, "ever-lasting Whig."[2] In an otherwise superior study, *Lincoln and the Economics of the American Dream* (1978), Gabor S. Boritt carried the Donald thesis to almost absurd lengths, contending that Lincoln was not only "the Whig in the White House," but that his military strategy itself—even his choice of generals—derived from his Whiggish economics.[3] In his prize-winning *Grant: A Biography* (1981), William S. McFeely took the Whig-in-the-White-House theme to its furthest extreme. Since Lincoln was a Whig, McFeely asserts, then it was Grant who became "the first truly Republican President."[4]

With all due respect, is this entire argument not a little preposterous? Lincoln was a *Republican* in the White House, not a Whig. Any attempt to make him into a Whig president, to borrow one of his lines, is "but a specious and fantastic arrangement of words, by which a man can prove a horse chestnut to be a chestnut horse."[5]

From the outset, the Whig thesis is predicated on the assumption that Lincoln left the Whigs reluctantly in 1856 and that ideologically he remained attached to the old party. This does not accord with the evidence. By 1856, he had become convinced that old party labels— even his own Whig label—severely impeded the mobilization of anti-extensionist forces and that a new free-soil party was imperative. The Republicans now loomed as the new major party of the future, and Lincoln readily enlisted in their crusade to contain the spread of slavery. In fact, he gave the keynote address for the formation of the Republican party in Illinois and went on to become its undisputed head. Lincoln never said, in a single surviving document, that he regretted the demise of the Whigs. Indeed, they had become obsolete in the battles over slavery that dominated the 1850s, and he left the old party with scarcely a backward glance.[6]

All his political life, it is true, Lincoln subscribed to the Whig principles of national unity and stability. All his political life, he championed the right of all Americans to rise, to harvest the full fruits of their labors, and to better themselves as their own talent and industry allowed.[7] When the Whig party died, these principles became the economic cornerstone of the Republican party, of former Democrats and Liberty men as well as former Whigs. And Lincoln was a Republican in propounding those principles.

Lincoln marched happily in Republican ranks because they afforded him an ideological home for all his principles, political as well as economic. In Republican ranks, he no longer had to consort with proslavery Southerners, as he had had to with the Whigs. In Republican ranks, he belonged to a party that forthrightly denounced slavery as a moral wrong and that shared Lincoln's views of the American experiment and the inalienable rights of man. He called himself a Republican, thought of himself as a Republican. In 1858, when national party leaders flirted with the idea of endorsing Stephen A. Douglas for the Senate, Lincoln became upset. Douglas is not your man for the Senate, he warned Republican leaders in the East. *I am your man. I, a pure Republican.*[8]

Indeed, nobody upheld Republican dogma more eloquently and unswervingly than Lincoln. No Republican was more determined to block the alleged Slave Power plot to make bondage powerful and permanent on these shores. No Republican was more passionate in his ringing denunciations of slavery as "a vast moral evil" and his equally ringing defenses of America's *"central idea"*—the idea of equality and the right to rise. No Republican was more committed to the principles of free labor, self-help, social mobility, and economic independence, all of which lay at the center of Republican ideology, of Lincoln's ideology. No Republican believed more strongly than he in the Republican vision of a future America, a better America than then existed: an America of thriving farms and bustling villages, an America of self-made agrarians, merchants, and shopkeepers who set examples and provided jobs for self-improving free workers—an America, however, that might never come about should slavery, class rule, and despotism triumph in Lincoln's impassioned time.[9]

When he ran for the presidency in 1860, Lincoln stood emphatically on the Republican platform of free soil, free labor, and free men. In offering him as their candidate, Republicans expected him to be a loyal party man who would defend the Republican cause without letting the standard down. He did not disappoint them. As party standard bearer, he opposed compromising Republican principles, opposed lowering the party platform "a hair's breadth" to let the likes of Douglas on it. Let Republicans resist slavery as a moral wrong regardless of the trials ahead, Lincoln had told his fellow Republicans. "LET US HAVE FAITH THAT MIGHT MAKES RIGHT. AND IN THAT FAITH, LET US, TO THE END, DARE TO DO OUR DUTY AS WE UNDERSTAND IT."[10] Small wonder that even the so-called radical Republicans extolled his addresses, applauded his nomination, and campaigned indefatigably in his behalf.

During the secession crisis, Lincoln remained an unyielding Republican. "Let there be no compromise on the question of *extending* slavery," he exhorted Republican leaders in Congress. "There is no possible compromise upon it, but which puts us under again, and leaves all our work to do over again." "We are not," he declared, going to let the Republican party "become 'a mere sucked egg, all shell and no meat,—the principle all sucked out.' " Directing congressional Republicans to "hold firm, as with a chain of steel," he rallied them to his side and won praise from Republican ranks. Lincoln was all right, said an enthusiastic Massachusetts Republican, because he kept the party firm and steady in its purpose.[11]

Nevertheless, the president-elect endorsed the idea of a limited chief executive when it came to the legislative process. "By the constitution," he said on his way to Washington, "the executive may recommend measures which he may think proper; and he may veto those he thinks improper; and it is supposed he may add to these, certain indirect influences to affect the action of Congress."[12] Lincoln added, however, that "my political education strongly inclines me against a very free use of any of these means, by the Executive, to control the legislation of the country. As a rule, I think it better that Congress should originate, as well as perfect its measures, without external bias."[13]

As a rule, he thought Congress ought to conduct its business without executive interference. What awaited him in Washington, however, was not the rule. What awaited him was a catastrophic civil war, a holocaust for which Lincoln, his party, and his country were totally unprepared, a tornado of blood and wreckage with Lincoln himself whirling in its center. What he did to quell the storm did not conform to some Whig theory about executive responsibility. No, he defined and fought the war according to his core of unshakable convictions about America's experiment in popular government and its historic mission in the progress of human liberty. In doing so, he remained a thoroughgoing Republican, deeply principled and yet flexible, willing to adopt new measures and stratagems in order to save the American experiment.

The central issue of the war, he told Congress on Independence Day 1861, was whether a constitutional republic—a system of popular government—could preserve itself. There were Europeans who argued that anarchy and rebellion were inherent weaknesses of a republic and that a monarchy was the more stable form of government. Now, in the Civil War, popular government was going through a fiery trial for its very survival. If it failed in America, if it succumbed to the forces of reaction in the world represented by the slave-based Confederacy, it might indeed perish from the earth. The beacon of hope for oppressed humanity would be destroyed. "This is essentially a People's contest," Lincoln said. "On the side of the Union, it is a struggle for maintaining in the world, that form, and substance of government, whose leading object is, to elevate the condition of men—to lift artificial weights from all shoulders—to clear the paths of laudable pursuit for all—to afford all, an unfettered start, and a fair chance, in the race of life."[14]

Yes, this was the central idea of the war. This was what Lincoln had in mind when he said "I shall do nothing in malice. What I deal with is too vast for malicious dealing." And in various ways he repeated that central idea in the difficult days that followed. They were fighting, he told crowds and visitors at the White House, to preserve something that lay at the heart of the American promise, at the heart of the Republican promise. "I happen temporarily to occupy this big White House," he said to an Ohio regiment. "I am a living witness that one of your children may look to come here as my father's child has. It is in order that each of you may have through this free government which we have enjoyed, an open field and a fair chance for your industry, enterprise and intelligence; that you may all have equal privileges in the race of life, with all its desirable human aspirations. It is for this the struggle should be maintained, that we may not lose our birthright."[15]

It was that idea that Lincoln fought for, that he kept uppermost in his mind, as the war dragged endlessly on. The war consumed him, demanding almost all his energy from dawn until late into the night. He had almost no time for his family, for recreation beyond a daily carriage ride, for meals and leisurely jokes and laughter with old friends, for government matters unrelated to the conflict. Every day, whenever he could spare a moment, Lincoln hurried to the telegraph office of the war department to get the latest military news. He was there during almost all the campaigns, pacing back and forth with his hands clasped behind him, sending out anxious telegraph messages to some southern battlefront. *What news now? What from Burnside? From Hooker? What goes?* He even brought documents to the telegraph office and worked on them at a borrowed desk. It was here, as he awaited military developments, that he wrote an early draft of his preliminary Emancipation Proclamation.

As I have argued elsewhere, the war and Lincoln's response to it defined him as a president. As the war grew and changed, so Lincoln grew and changed. At first, he warned that the conflict must not turn into a "remorseless revolutionary struggle," lest that cause vast social and political wreckage.[16] As a consequence, his initial war strategies were cautious and limited. But when the conflict ground on with no end in sight, Lincoln resorted to one harsh war measure after another to subdue the rebellion and save popular government: he embraced martial law, property confiscation, emancipation, Negro troops, conscription, and scorched-earth warfare, all of which most of the so-called radical Republicans had urged on him. These turned the war into the very thing he had cautioned against: a remorseless revolutionary struggle whose concussions are still being felt. And it became such a struggle because of Lincoln's unswerving commitment to the war's central idea.[17]

That idea, and the practical demands of the war, dictated Lincoln's dealings with his cabinet and with Congress. In cabinet matters, our Republican president did indeed delegate authority, allowing his secretaries broad discretionary powers in running their departments. But not because Whig theory informed him that this was what William Henry Harrison and Zachary Taylor would have done. Lincoln delegated authority because he simply did not have time to do everything himself. He may have been an extraordinary man, but he was not superman. He also delegated authority because his secretaries, after he got rid of Simon Cameron, were all capable subordinates whose talents he needed.

But if Lincoln allowed his secretaries considerable latitude in handling their affairs, he scarcely let them dominate him. When Secretary of State William H. Seward offered to take over the administration in April 1861, Lincoln put him firmly in his place. "Executive force and vigor are rare qualities," Seward confided to his wife. "The President is the best of us."[18]

Charged with the awesome task of managing the government in the midst of a huge and confusing war, of supervising federal armies of unprecedented size, of searching for generals who knew how to fight, of trying to deal with the crucial slavery problem and the issue of race that underlay it, of coping with a stream of raucous humanity that poured daily through his office, of somehow keeping sight of the historic and global dimensions of the conflict, Lincoln became a tough administrator indeed. "I never knew with what tyrannous authority he runs the Cabinet, till now," John Hay recorded in the summer of 1863. "The most important things he decides & there is no cavil." "He will not be bullied—even by his friends."[19]

As with the cabinet, Lincoln's relationship with Congress depended almost entirely on the pressures and problems of the war, not on Whig voices whispering in his head about what a good president ought to do. True, as Donald says, Lincoln seldom used his veto power and had little connection with the procession of economic legislation coming out of the wartime Capitol. Not that Lincoln lacked interest in such measures. On the contrary, they implemented his own national economic outlook—they promoted the "material growth of the nation" and the rise of the "many," and so were related to the war's central idea. Yet he was too preoccupied with the war and the very survival of popular government to propose economic legislation. As Boritt conceded, economics in wartime—to use a Lincoln saying—seemed "small potatoes and too few in a hill."[20]

Even so, Lincoln maintained close ties with Congress, for he needed its support if the war was to be won and the future of popular government guaranteed. As a consequence, he disregarded what he had once said about how legislators should function without executive bias. It was to Congress, significantly, that Lincoln explained the central idea of the war. It was to Congress that he turned for reform legislation linked to that idea. Shocked by the Sioux war in Minnesota and reports that a corrupt Indian Office was to blame, Lincoln urged Congress to remodel the Indian system so as to avoid fraud and conflicts that only besmirched the American experiment.[21] It was to Congress, moreover, that Lincoln submitted his federal-state emancipation scheme of 1862, to Congress that he recommended a constitutional amendment that would abolish American slavery forever, to Congress that he outlined his ten percent plan of reconstruction.

What was more, it was Lincoln who helped Senator Charles Sumner of Massachusetts guide through Congress a bill that granted widows and orphans of slave soldiers the same benefits as whites; Lincoln who pressed Congress to approve his reconstructed governments in Louisiana and Arkansas; Lincoln who forged with Sumner and other so-called radical Republicans a compromise that would have permitted Negro enfranchisement in other conquered rebel states if Congress would accept his Louisiana regime; Lincoln who employed all the pressure and prestige of his office to get the present Thirteenth Amendment through a recalcitrant House of Representatives. With the outcome much in doubt, Lincoln and congressional Republicans participated in secret negotiations never made public—negotiations that allegedly involved patronage, a New Jersey railroad monopoly, and the release of rebels related to congressional Democrats—to bring wavering opponents into line. "The greatest measure of the nineteenth century," Thaddeus Stevens claimed, "was passed by corruption, aided and abetted by the purest man in America."[22]

Lincoln dealt with Congress in other ways, too. Throughout the war he consulted with numerous individual congressmen, seeking advice on all matter of war problems from military developments to emancipation and diplomacy. As Donald himself has demonstrated, Lincoln made Senator Sumner one of his major foreign-policy advisers, and Sumner in turn became a loyal Lincoln man on Capitol Hill until breaking with the president over reconstruction.[23] In addition to Sumner, Lincoln maintained personal contact with the Joint Committee on the Conduct of the War, composed mainly of hard-line Republicans, whose job it was to ferret out disloyalists and incompetents in both the administration and the military. Lincoln met frequently with the worried patriots who served on the committee, hearing out their complaints about generals and cabinet members and even listening to criticisms of his own war policies. The president and the committeemen often disagreed, sometimes emphatically, but they had a mutual regard for one another and kept the lines of communication open between the White House and Capitol Hill.

In his reconstruction efforts, as I have indicated, Lincoln also sought Congress's approval and cooperation, for he acknowledged that Capitol Hill had a powerful voice in the reconstruction process, since both houses would decide whether to accept representatives from the states he restored. He did clash with Republicans like Sumner, Stevens, and Benjamin Wade, who argued that reconstruction was a congressional and not a presidential responsibility. Sumner also opposed Lincoln's military approach because he did not understand how the army could produce an American state. But, despite their differences, Lincoln and congressional Republicans stood together on most crucial reconstruction issues. They agreed that the South must be remade. They meant to abolish slavery there forever. They were concerned about the welfare of the freedmen. And they intended for southern Unionists to rule in postwar Dixie. Above all, they wanted to prevent ex-Confederate leaders from taking over the postwar South and forming a coalition with northern Democrats that might imperil the gains of the war. Lincoln and his congressional associates often disagreed on how to implement their goals—nearly all congressional Republicans, for example, demanded a tougher loyalty oath than that required by the president's ten percent plan.[24] But even so, the president and congressional Republicans retained a close and mutually respectful relationship, so much so that many contemporaries thought they would remain as united in working out reconstruction problems as they had been in prosecuting the war.[25]

In sum, far from deferring weakly to Congress except in matters of military necessity, Lincoln sought to influence Capitol Hill, to pressure, cajole, consult, and work with his Republican colleagues there, on virtually all issues involving the war and its central idea: the salvation of popular government and the right of all Americans to rise. Clearly this was no latter-day Whig in the White House. It was no Whig who wrote those magnificent state papers about the purpose of the war and the mission of the American experiment. It was no Whig who responded to the entreaties of Republicans like Sumner, defied public opinion, and issued the Emancipation Proclamation—the most revolutionary measure to come from an American president up to that time. It was no Whig who raised Republican ideology to the lofty heights of the Gettysburg Address, giving here the eloquent defense of liberty that critics often find lacking in the proclamation. It was no Whig who delivered the lyrical second inaugural, singing out that God perhaps had willed this "mighty scourge of war" on North and South alike, "until all the wealth piled by the bondman's two hundred and fifty years of unrequited toil shall be sunk, and until every drop drawn with the lash, shall be paid by another drawn with the sword."[26]

Nor was it a Whig who in April 1865 was prepared to reconstruct the South with the help of an occupying army. It was no Whig who desired to reform and reshape the South's shattered society in accordance with the ideals of the Republican party: to bring the South into the mainstream of American republicanism, to install a free-labor system there for blacks as well as whites, to establish public schools for both races, to look after the welfare of the former slaves, to grant them access to the ballot and the courts—in short, to build a new South dedicated like Lincoln to the Declaration of Independence and the preservation of popular government. It was no Whig who had fought the war through to a total Union triumph and a larger concept of the inalienable rights of man that now included the American Negro. It was no Whig who had summoned Americans both North and South, Americans both black and white, to dedicate themselves to a new birth of freedom, so that government of, by, and for *all* the people would not perish from the earth. No, the man who did all that was a principled and dedicated Republican, and he deserves to be remembered that way.

NOTES

1 / David Donald, *Lincoln Reconsidered: Essays on the Civil War Era*, paperback ed. (New York, 1956), 187–208.

2 / Kenneth Stampp, *The Era of Reconstruction, 1865–1877* (New York, 1965), 25–49.

3 / Gabor S. Boritt, *Lincoln and the Economics of the American Dream* (Memphis, Tenn., 1978), 195–231, 267–74.

4 / McFeely, *Grant: A Biography* (New York, 1981), 292. In his review of *Grant* in the *New Republic* (February 28, 1981), Justin Kaplan, alas, repeats McFeely's assertion as gospel.

5 / *The Collected Works of Abraham Lincoln,* ed. Roy P. Basler, Marion Delores Pratt, and Lloyd A. Dunlap, 9 vols. (New Brunswick, N.J., 1953–55), 3:16.

6 / Don E. Fehrenbacher, *Prelude to Greatness: Lincoln in the 1850's* (Stanford, Calif., 1962), 44–47, 86. For a history of Lincoln's keynote address at Bloomington, see Elwell Crissey, *Lincoln's Lost Speech* (New York, 1967).

7 / See Boritt, *Lincoln and the Economics of the American Dream,* ix and passim; and Stephen B. Oates, *Abraham Lincoln: The Man behind the Myths* (New York, 1984), 59–60.

8 / See Stephen B. Oates, *With Malice Toward None: The Life of Abraham Lincoln* (New York, 1977), 127–40.

9 / *Collected Works of Lincoln,* 2:494, 385; 3:462–63, 477–81; and *The Collected Works of Abraham Lincoln—Supplement, 1832–1865,* ed. Roy P. Basler (Westport, Conn., 1974), 43–45. For Republican thought, see Eric Foner, *Free Soil, Free Labor, Free Men: The Ideology of the Republican Party before the Civil War* (New York, 1970).

10 / *Collected Works of Lincoln,* 3:547–50.

11 / Ibid., 4:149–50, 151–54, 183; *The Letters of Henry Adams,* ed. Worthington Chauncey Ford (Boston and New York, 1930), 68–69; David M. Potter, *Lincoln and His Party in the Secession Crisis* (New Haven and London, 1942), 156–61.

12 / *Collected Works of Lincoln,* 4:214. Donald wrongly paraphrases Lincoln's remarks, thereby making it appear that he "did not believe" that the executive should exercise his constitutional prerogatives at all (*Lincoln Reconsidered,* 199).

13 / *Collected Works of Lincoln,* 4:214.

14 / Ibid., 4:438.

15 / Ibid., 5:346; 7:512.

16 / Ibid., 5:49.

17 / For an elaboration, see Oates, *Lincoln: Man behind the Myths,* 89–147.

18 / Quoted in Benjamin P. Thomas, *Abraham Lincoln* (New York, 1952), 254.

19 / Tyler Dennett, ed., *Lincoln and the Civil War in the Diaries and Letters of John Hay* (1939; reprint ed., Westport, Conn., 1972), 76; Helen Nicolay, *Lincoln's Secretary: A Biography of John G. Nicolay* (New York, 1949), 83.

20 / David Homer Bates, *Lincoln in the Telegraph Office* (New York, 1907), 266; Boritt, *Lincoln and the Economics of the American Dream,* 231.

21 / Lincoln, however, was up against powerful congressional elements with a vested interest in retaining the nefarious Indian system the way it was. In the end, Congress rejected Lincoln's call for reform, and the president turned back to the war. Still, there can be no doubt that he intended to do something about the Indian system when he had the opportunity. As he said (and meant): "If we get through this war, and I live, *this Indian system shall be reformed.*" See David A. Nichols, *Lincoln and the Indians: Civil War Policy and Politics* (Columbia, Mo., and London, 1978), 94–118, 129–46, 148.

22 / Quoted in Fawn M. Brodie, *Thaddeus Stevens, Scourge of the South* (New York, 1959), 204.

23 / David Donald, *Charles Sumner and the Rights of Man* (New York, 1970), 19ff.

24 / For Lincoln's closeness to congressional Republicans, see Peyton McCrary, *Abraham Lincoln and Reconstruction: The Louisiana Experiment* (Princeton, 1978), 3–15; Donald, *Charles Sumner and the Rights of Man,* 207–8; Harold M. Hyman, *A More Perfect Union: The Impact of the Civil War and Reconstruction on the Constitution,* paperback ed. (Boston, 1975), 276–81, and Hyman, *Lincoln's Reconstruction: Neither Failure of Vision nor Vision of Failure,* the third R. Gerald McMurtry Lecture, Fort Wayne, Ind., May 8, 1980; Herman Belz, *Reconstructing the Union: Theory and Policy During the Civil War* (Ithaca, N.Y., 1969), 309–10; Hans L. Trefousse, *The Radical Republicans: Lincoln's Vanguard for*

Racial Justice (New York, 1969), 286–304; and Oates, *Lincoln: Man behind the Myths,* 141–46.

25 / George W. Julian, Isaac Arnold, and Hugh McCulloch all thought so. See Belz, *Reconstructing the Union,* 309–10.

26 / *Collected Works of Lincoln,* 8:333.

MICHAEL F. HOLT

★

Abraham Lincoln and the Politics of Union

ONE OF THE MOST STIMULATING ANALYSES OF CIVIL WAR politics ever written is a brilliant essay by Eric McKitrick called "Party Politics and the Union and Confederate War Efforts."[1] In it, McKitrick argues that the North had a decisive advantage over the South because it continued to have two-party rivalry during the war while the Confederacy did not. The presence of the Democratic party forced Republicans of all kinds to rally behind the policies of the Republican government to win elections. As a result, the North remained more united during the long ordeal than the division-plagued Confederacy.

According to McKitrick, party politics also made Abraham Lincoln a more effective presidential leader than his Confederate counterpart, Jefferson Davis. The organization and partisan needs of the Republican party provided Lincoln with guidelines, first to select and then to reshuffle his cabinet, with ways to ensure the loyalty of his vice presidents, with incentives to gain the cooperation of state governors, and with sanctions to punish political opponents both inside and outside his own party. In contrast, the hapless Davis lacked party lines to separate friends from foes and to generate institutional loyalty to his administration. Hence he could not control his cabinet, Vice President Alexander Stephens, obstreperous governors like Joe Brown of Georgia and Zeb

Vance of North Carolina, or political opponents in Congress and the electorate. McKitrick concludes that it was because of the presence of a two-party system that Lincoln was able to hold the North together long enough to win the war. Without the glue that parties provided, Davis could not prevent centrifugal forces from tearing the Confederacy apart.

Despite the stunning originality of McKitrick's argument, it leaves several crucial questions unanswered. Most important, it slights the critical matter of Lincoln's relationship with the Republican majority in Congress. If the presence of the Democratic opposition pressured Republicans to pull together, how can one explain the well-known hostility of many Republicans to Lincoln, the effort of Republican senators to purge his favorite William Henry Seward from the cabinet, or the palpable conflict between Lincoln and the congressional wing of his party over emancipation, the arming of blacks, reconstruction, and other wartime policies?

Once it was fashionable to blame these clashes on a cabal of vindictive radicals who frustrated the benevolent plans of the magnanimous president. Now we know that such a melodramatic interpretation is misleading. Although there were indeed radical and moderate factions in the Republican party during the war, virtually all congressional Republicans, not just the radicals, blamed Lincoln for failing to prosecute the war vigorously enough and to move against slavery rapidly enough, and virtually all voted for the measures that set Congress's policy apart from Lincoln's. Nor is it satisfactory to contend, as some historians have, that Lincoln and congressional Republicans had the same fundamental goals, that they were traveling the same road at different rates, and that Lincoln was really happy to have the more radical congressmen blaze the trail. Timing is almost everything in politics, and that line of argument fails to explain why Lincoln and Congress wanted to move at different speeds while it simultaneously minimizes the seriousness of the disputes between them. Finally, it is not terribly convincing to assert that the pragmatic and sagacious Lincoln, alone among the Republican politicians in Washington, recognized the need to keep the border slave states and northern Democrats behind the war effort and therefore resisted congressional demands concerning emancipation and the use of black troops that might alienate them. Lincoln had no monopoly on political wisdom or common sense. Congressional Republicans must have recognized the potential political impact of the policies they advocated. Nonetheless, they vigorously demanded them, often against Lincoln's wishes. Why?[2]

This essay suggests that the continuation of the two-party system, which McKitrick sees as the cause of Republican unity during the war, was in fact the source of the division between Lincoln and Congress over wartime policy. Because Lincoln and congressional Republicans adopted different political strategies in response to the challenge posed by the Democratic party, they also pursued different paths to fight the war they both wanted to win. The result of Congress going one way and Lincoln another, however, was a more successful war effort than the North would have achieved had it followed either course alone. McKitrick may not be correct about the precise way in which a two-party system helped the northern war effort, but he is correct about the result. It significantly contributed to northern victory.[3]

To understand Civil War politics it is necessary to remember three facts of political life. First, the Democratic party remained a potent challenger to Republicans in the North. Though divided between two candidates and forced to defend one of the most unpopular and corrupt administrations in American history, the Democrats still won almost 44 percent of the popular vote in the free states in 1860. As the war progressed, moreover, controversial Republican policies like emancipation, conscription, and the suspension of *habeas corpus* gave them golden issues to campaign on. The menace of a Democratic comeback, in sum, was no chimera.

Second, the Republican party had no base of any consequence in any slave state. In 1860 Lincoln's support in the border states that remained in the Union ranged from 24 percent in tiny Delaware to a pitiful 1 percent in his native Kentucky. In the slave states that seceded Lincoln received a handful of votes only in Virginia; no Republican tickets had even been distributed in the other ten states that joined the Confederacy. It may strike some as odd to include Confederate states in a discussion of the political situation that shaped the clash between Lincoln and congressional Republicans, but one must remember that the fundamental northern purpose in the war was to restore those states to the Union. Certainly Lincoln hoped they would be voting again in the congressional and presidential elections of 1864, if not earlier, and they seemed likely to vote against Lincoln and other Republican candidates unless support were developed within them.

Third, and most important, Lincoln and congressional Republicans had different constituencies. Lincoln faced a national electorate, not a local one, and he had won less than 40 percent of the popular vote in 1860. To achieve reelection he had to worry about winning statewide pluralities both in the free states, where the race had often been close even in 1860 when the opposition divided among three candidates, and in the border and Confederate slave states, where he had virtually no organizational or popular support. There is no need to question Lincoln's desire for reelection. Virtually everyone who knew him commented on his insatiable political ambition. Like most politicians, moreover, Lincoln convinced himself that his reelection was in the best interest of the nation and that the political strategy he pursued to achieve it was the best way to restore the Union.

Unlike Lincoln, congressional Republicans did not have to consider areas of existing or potential Democratic strength in their own political calculations. By definition the vast majority of them came from districts where the Republican party was strongest and most secure from the Democratic challenge. Most of them, that is, received a larger proportion of the vote in their local congressional districts than Lincoln did of the statewide vote in their states, especially in the hotly contested battlegrounds of Illinois, Indiana, Ohio, and New York (see table 1). To such men the campaign formula that had brought Republicans to power in the late 1850s seemed perfectly capable of keeping them in power in the 1860s. That strategy was to denounce southern political power as unfair and dangerous, to expose a supposed Slave Power conspiracy against northern liberties, to arraign northern Democrats for complicity in that southern plot, and to promise to eradicate that southern threat once Republicans achieved power.[4] In short, Republican congressmen believed that they had won office in the past and could win again in the future by running as an antisouthern party.

Because they had different constituencies, Lincoln and Republican congressmen reacted differently to the problems posed by the Democratic opposition and the conduct of the war. Usually familiar with public opinion only in the staunchest Republican strongholds, congressional Republicans believed their constituents demanded a ruthless, no-holds-barred crusade to crush the South and humble the Slave Power. Aghast at reports that northern generals protected civilian property in the South, an Ohio Republican senator ranted in 1862, for example, that "this was not the way in which the people desired the war to be conducted, and . . . [that] generals were trying the patience of the country too far." Before the people of the North would accept a Confederate victory, a New Jersey Republican congressman vowed, "they will arm every slave against his rebel master; will drive the whole white population beyond the borders; and hold the once proud states . . . as Territories for the home of the enfranchised negro."[5] Republican congressmen were therefore convinced that what was best for their own prospects of reelection, for the Republican party as a whole, and for the

Table 1 / Lincoln's Percentage of the Popular Vote in 1860 Compared to the Percentage of the Popular Vote Won by Victorious Republican Congressional Candidates in Northern States in 1860 and 1861[a]

		Congress	
	Lincoln	Median	Average
Maine	64%	55.3%	56.7%
New Hampshire	57	52.8	53.1 (1861)
Vermont	75	75.2	75.7
Massachusetts	62.5	64	63.7
Connecticut	54	53.7	53.7 (1861)
New York	53.7	58.8	57.5
New Jersey	48	52.7	52.7
Pennsylvania	56	54.2	57.2
Ohio	52.3	57.2	58.2
Indiana	51.1	54.5	55.4
Illinois	50.7	62.2	62.5
Michigan	57.1	57.5	57
Iowa	55.1	55.2	55.2
Wisconsin	56.5	54.5	56.5
California	32.2		
Oregon	37.9		

[a]This table includes congressional percentages only for victorious Republican candidates, not for all candidates. Returns were taken from the *Tribune Almanac*, which listed no popular results for congressional races in California and Oregon.

nation was the most vigorous prosecution possible of the war against the Confederacy. Hence Congress constantly thrust powers on Lincoln he was reluctant to use and insisted on the retention of fugitive slaves who fled to Union armies, the confiscation of rebel property, emancipation, the enlistment of black troops, conscription, test oaths, and a host of other measures it believed necessary to win the war and punish the planter aristocracy.

That Democrats protested many of their measures worried most congressional Republicans not a whit. Except for a few Republicans who had slipped into office in 1860 and 1861 with a minority of the vote in multicandidate races,[6] they were relatively immune to Democratic efforts to exploit resentment at their actions because of the strength of the party in their own districts. Besides, Democratic opposition allowed Republicans to continue to portray northern Democrats as allies of the Slave Power. In their eyes, in short, harsh antisouthern measures would not only help win the war; they would also provide a platform to help Republicans win elections.

Nor, so long as Republicans maintained majorities in Congress and northern state legislatures, were congressional Republicans concerned that their policies might strengthen Democrats outside their own strongholds. After all, they personally did not have to run in such areas. On the other hand, they would brook no serious threat to their own hold on state and national governments. They bitterly protested the appointment of Democrats as civilian or military leaders of the war effort. They also tried to deny power to or strip effective power from offices and jurisdictions that Democrats controlled. In January 1862, for example, Republicans expelled the Indiana Democrat Jesse Bright from the Senate on the flimsiest of pretexts. Similarly, when Democrats captured a number of northern legislatures and the governorship of New York and New Jersey in the fall of 1862, Republicans rushed the most nationalistic legislation of the war through Congress between December 1862 and March 1863. The explicit purpose of the National Banking Act, the draft, and the Habeas Corpus-Indemnity-Removal Act was to shift control of banking, manpower, and legal suits against federal officials from state governments which Democrats now controlled to the national government which Republicans still dominated.

This same unwillingness to see Democrats exercise power, finally, explains the Republicans' hostility to a rapid readmission of Confederate states to political rights. Those states seemed sure to aid the Democrats whatever the nominal partisan affiliation of the men they sent to Congress. "What!" an Illinois Republican protested in February 1862, "Bring back the rebel States into full fellowship as members of the union, with their full delegations in both Houses of Congress. They, with the pro-slavery conservatives of the Border States and the Democrats of the Northern states, will control Congress. Republicans and Republican principles will be in the minority. . . ." As early as January 1863, therefore, the Republican caucus in the House determined not to seat men elected from occupied Confederate states. So too they fought Lincoln's ten percent plan, attempted to substitute the more rigorous Wade-Davis bill that would delay restoration, and resisted the readmission of Louisiana until after Lincoln died.[7]

Congressional Republicans, in sum, approached the military conflict with the Confederacy and the political conflict with the Democracy in exactly the same way. In neither would they make concessions to induce cooperation; in neither did they seek compromise or accommodation. In both they demanded war to the hilt.

Lincoln's responses to the Democratic and Confederate challenges were dramatically different. Consolidating the Republican party in its existing strongholds by baiting Democrats and humiliating the South did little to improve his personal prospects for reelection. He could not afford to alienate non–Republicans in the northern, border-state, and Confederate areas outside of those established bastions. His solution was not to confront Democrats with distinctively Republican policies or to deny Democratic areas the power they deserved. Instead he attempted to build a new coalition under his leadership that included pro-slavery conservatives from the border states, northern Democrats, and former rebels from the Confederacy, just the groups congressional Republicans feared would put Republican principles in the minority. This was *not* simply a matter of broadening the base of the Republican party as some historians have maintained. Rather it was an attempt to replace the Republican party with a new bisectional organization to be called the Union party.

To state the argument most boldly, Lincoln almost from the moment he was elected set out to destroy the Republican party as it existed in 1860, that is, as an exclusively northern party whose sole basis of cohesion was hostility toward the South and the Democratic party.

Instead, Lincoln wanted to create a new national coalition with support in both sections, a party built around the issue of restoring the Union, rather than the issue of crushing the Slave Power or abolishing slavery as congressional Republicans wanted. To achieve his own political goal, in short, Lincoln had to jettison the antisouthern platform that congressional Republicans insisted on retaining.

Some years ago David Donald suggested that Lincoln's actions as president reflected his political upbringing, that he was an exemplary Whig in the White House because he deferred to Congress on virtually all nonmilitary legislation.[8] In attempting to change the name, the program, and the constituency of the party that elected him, Lincoln also acted like a good Whig. All of his Whig predecessors in the office—John Tyler, Zachary Taylor, and Millard Fillmore—had tried to create a new party to replace the Whig party that had put them in office. As Lincoln would during the Civil War, moreover, they too had met fierce hostility from the congressional wing of their party because congressmen wanted to perpetuate rather than abandon the existing organization.

Lincoln clearly hoped to enhance his chances for reelection by forging a new party that would broaden support for him in the North and marshal it in the South. But personal political expediency alone did not dictate his course. Lincoln's lifelong beliefs about the nature of the American republic also impelled him toward the same solution. Perhaps no politician has ever articulated so elegantly and succinctly as Lincoln the fundamental premise of American republicanism, that ours is a government of the people, by the people, and for the people. And the people exercised self-government, he believed, through the votes they cast at elections. As he argued in his message to Congress in July 1861, for example, the purpose of the war was to demonstrate "that ballots are the rightful, and peaceful, successors of bullets; and that when ballots have fairly, and constitutionally, decided, there can be no successful appeal back to bullets; that there can be no successful appeal, except to ballots themselves, at succeeding elections."[9]

For Lincoln, then, the restoration of the Confederate states to the Union was preeminently a political process, a matter of the people of those states going to the polls and voting to return to the Union. Almost as soon as Yankee armies secured various parts of the South, therefore, Lincoln pressed his military governors to hold elections. "If we could somehow, get a vote of the people of Tennessee and have it result properly," he wrote Andrew Johnson on July 3, 1862, "it would be worth more to us than a battle gained." Throughout the war, indeed, Lincoln wheedled, cajoled, and threatened Southerners in attempts to induce them to vote themselves back into the Union. The major purpose of Lincoln's preliminary emancipation proclamation in September 1862, for example, was not to appease congressional Republicans or European governments or even to prepare the way for actual abolition. Rather it was to pressure Confederates to hold elections before January 1, 1863, in order to avoid emancipation. Lincoln made his purpose clear when he ordered his military governors in Louisiana, Tennessee, Arkansas, and North Carolina to arrange elections before that date to demonstrate the fidelity to the Union of those occupied areas. When the army commander in eastern Virginia specifically asked Lincoln if occupied areas that held congressional elections would be exempted from emancipation, Lincoln, referring to the proclamation, replied, "It is obvious to all that I therein intended to give time and opportunity. Also it is seen I left myself at liberty to exempt *parts* of states. Without saying more, I shall be very glad if any Congressional District will, in good faith, do as your dispatch contemplates." Similarly, Lincoln's famous amnesty proclamation and ten percent plan of December 1863 were meant to hasten the holding of elections to restore southern states by creating an electorate to vote in them, a policy at odds with the wishes of congressional Republicans. In short, while congressional Republicans wanted to subdue the Confederacy with bullets, Lincoln wanted to redeem it with ballots cast by Southerners themselves.[10]

Lincoln realized, moreover, that for elections in occupied areas to "result properly," Southerners needed something more tangible to vote for than the mere idea of reunion. They had to elect politicians who would establish loyal state governments. For those politicians to be able to retain political control of their states against pro-Confederate elements within them, in turn, voter support had to be institutionalized. Since those pro-Confederate elements were overwhelmingly Democratic, finally, Lincoln had to establish a new anti-Democratic political party in the South in order to achieve reconstruction through the political process as he desired.

Such a party, however, could not be called or even allied with the Republican party as long as the congressional Republicans pursued the harsh antisouthern policies they favored. Events in the South after the collapse of the Whig party in the mid-1850s had demonstrated that no matter how much southern voters and politicians disliked Democrats, they would not and could not support a palpably antisouthern party like the Republicans. Instead they had been compelled to join southern Democrats in denouncing the Republicans while simultaneously attempting to rally opposition to the Democrats through a series of ephemeral non-Republican, anti-Democratic organizations, the most recent of which had been the Constitutional Union party which supported John Bell for president in 1860.[11]

Yet as long as anti-Democratic voters in the South were organized in a different party than Lincoln's own, they would not enhance his chances for reelection against the Democrats once Confederate states returned to the Union. Nor could such a party secure the permanent restoration of the South that Lincoln sought. The course of political history in the antebellum South had demonstrated that no party could survive in the region unless it was an authentic national party with a northern wing, a party with a genuine chance to win the presidency and control Congress.[12] To build a successful anti-Confederate, pro-reunion party in the Confederate states, in short, Lincoln also had to replace the Republicans with a more palatable anti-Democratic party in the North, one that could serve as the northern wing of the party he needed in the South—at least as long as the southern electorate was confined to whites. Both to further his own chances for reelection in 1864 and to effect reunion, therefore, Lincoln attempted to jettison the name and the antisouthern program of the Republicans and to build a new Union party attractive to non-Republicans in both sections.

To understand why Lincoln believed he could accomplish this feat, one must appreciate that few people in the 1850s and 1860s anticipated that the Republicans would remain the permanent successors to the Whigs as the major anti-Democratic party in American politics. Accustomed to twenty years of bisectional interparty competition between Democrats and Whigs, many regarded the exclusively northern Republican party as a temporary aberration. As a result, proposals for displacing the Republicans with other anti-Democratic parties that eschewed sectionally oriented attacks on the South had abounded in the late 1850s. For example, it had required a terrific struggle for Republicans to overcome the Know-Nothing challenge to their credentials as the new anti-Democratic party in 1855–56, and they had been forced to beat back another attempt to launch a conservative, bisectional anti-Democratic party in 1858–59. Although John Bell's Constitutional Union candidacy had fared poorly against Lincoln in the free states in 1860, his virtual monopoly of the anti-Democratic vote in the slave states reaffirmed the potential that a different, non-Republican opposition party might have if it could secure that southern support.

The precarious position of the Republican party in certain northern states at the end of 1860 also encouraged Lincoln to hope that most Republicans might go along with his attempts to refashion the party. The Republicans carried California and Oregon in 1860 and again in 1861, for example, with less than 40 percent of the vote because the majority Democrats were divided into pronorthern and prosouthern wings. Republicans from such states might well see the wisdom of combining with the pro-Union wing of the Democracy. Republicans from Ohio, Illinois, Indiana, and New York where the 1860 race had been exceedingly close might also acquiesce in a change of name and platform that could add Bell men and some Democrats to their column. Such a change might be especially appealing to his supporters in New Jersey and Pennsylvania who did not even dare call themselves Republicans because of the antislavery, antisouthern connotations of the name. Instead they assumed the label "People's Party" which, as its adherents in Pennsylvania repeatedly told Lincoln, was decidedly different from the Republican party. "The Party in Pennsylvania are thoroughly *Anti* Abolitionist," wrote a Philadelphian, "and it is [only] with difficulty [that] we can keep them solid with the *Republican* party." Lincoln must not "give the *negro* question too much prominency," he added, "or I fear a reaction which will again throw our State into the ranks of the Democrats." When congressmen from Pennsylvania and other northern states urged Lincoln in the weeks following his election to appoint John Bell and other southern Constitutional Union men to the cabinet in order to effect a merger between the Republicans and "the Union element of the South" in the next Congress where Republicans expected to be in the minority, Lincoln's belief that he could fundamentally transform the party must have been strengthened.[13]

Political developments in the North and the South during the secession winter of 1860–61 both cemented that conviction and inspired the name and platform of the party Lincoln attempted to build during the war. Throughout the South in the elections to choose delegates to secession conventions, a voter realignment seemed to begin as Douglas Democrats and some nonslaveholding Breckinridge Democrats joined Constitutional Unionists in opposing immediate secession. In the upper South where these antisecession coalitions prevailed, they quickly moved to form Union parties to contest the congressional, gubernatorial, and state legislative elections scheduled for the spring, summer, and fall of 1861 against the remaining Democrats who favored secession.[14]

Almost immediately these southern Unionists contacted high-ranking Republicans like William Henry Seward, Thurlow Weed, Thomas Corwin, and Lincoln himself, begging them to drop their antisouthern stance and to join the Southerners in a new national Union party. Such a new party was necessary, they insisted, because the issue was no longer slavery's expansion versus free soil or North versus South, the dichotomies that had defined the Republican/Democratic rivalry of the late 1850s. Now the only issue was union or disunion.

Hence John Gilmer of North Carolina, whom Lincoln fervently wanted in his cabinet, advised the president-elect in December 1860 to disregard extremist Republicans when he formulated policies and "to come as far South as you can. You may divide from your many party friends, but by the preservation of the peace of the country, you will nationalize yourself and your party." Similarly, in January 1861 Gilmer urged the New York Republican boss Weed to help build "a great national party." In February the *Richmond Whig* concluded in a widely reprinted editorial that "the conservative Whigs and Democrats of the South and the conservative Republicans of the North must unite to form a new Union party."

> We predict that before the 4th of July this will be the arrangement of parties. The Republican party cannot exist in its present basis. Lincoln and Seward will have the sagacity to see this, and they will promptly give the cold shoulder to the extreme men of their party and try to establish a national party, which will repudiate the wild absurdities of the Abolition school. A political necessity will constrain them to abandon not only the extreme dogmas of their party, but also to adopt a new name significant of the policy of the new party, and this name must be the UNION PARTY.[15]

Before Lincoln's inauguration a number of northern Republicans appeared receptive to the idea. The Washington correspondent of the *New York Times* wrote in February 1861: "The question pending is one as to whether Mr. Lincoln shall become the head of the great 'Union Party' of the country, or whether a party upon that issue shall be permitted to grow up in hostility to his Administration." The incoming administration, he added, must choose between "the party issues of the *past*" and "the necessities of the future." Earlier that paper's editor, Henry J. Raymond, had privately advised Lincoln that "the Union men of the South must belong to our party—and it seems to me important that we should open the door to them as wide as the hinges will let it swing." In the present crisis, a founder of Ohio's Republican party warned, Lincoln must rally men of all parties who were loyal to the Union and not just Republicans. To do that, he must exclude from his administration "men, however worthy and prominent, who would be objectionable to the friends of the Union in other parties." Similarly, John Defrees, editor of the principal Republican newspaper in Indiana, wrote Lincoln that " 'Union' or 'dis-union' will soon be the division of the parties North and South, and your administration must be sustained by the Union men North and South." Appointing Southerners like John Bell to the cabinet would not only "build up a party" that would sustain Lincoln in the South, but it would "give us even additional strength in the North by bringing to us moderate Douglas men." "Some of our radicals might object," he confessed, "but most of them would soon be convinced of the wisdom of the movement."[16]

This last prediction proved erroneous. Even before the culmination of secession, many Republicans protested against any abandonment of Republican principles, "the party issues of the *past*" as the *Times* reporter had called them, to appease the South or any attempt to attract Southerners and northern Democrats to the party through patronage appointments. Thus a dismayed Indiana Republican asked his congressman in January 1861, "Is there not a movement . . . to build a 'union party' in the north which shall absorb Americans and Douglas men and Conservative Republicans; done for the purpose of killing what they term the Abolition element in the Republican party, aimed at men of our Stamp? The movement cannot amount to anything unless it should be the disruption of the Republican party."[17]

The completion of secession and outbreak of warfare widened Republican opposition to changing the party. Secession manifestly meant that attempts to deter it by wooing Southerners had failed. More important, the withdrawal of Southerners meant that Republicans could dominate Congress without southern support. War against the Confederacy, finally, offered an opportunity to build a platform of concrete antisouthern actions, actions they could not have taken against the Slave Power without the excuse the war provided. However amenable some Republicans had been to changing the image and broadening the constituency of the party in the winter of 1860–61, therefore, few remained so six months later. Instead of worrying about extending the party to the South, they focused throughout the war on consolidating its power in the North, a project that seemed to require no change in the party's image or constituency whatsoever.

Nonetheless, as is well known, during the war Lincoln's party did exchange the Republican name for the Union label, first at the state level in 1861, 1862, and 1863 and then at the party's national convention in 1864. Most historians, echoing contemporary Democrats, have regarded this action as a transparently cosmetic attempt by cynical Republicans to lure gullible Democrats and Unionists into supporting Republican candidates and Republican policies, not a genuine transformation of the party's constituency and principles. We in fact know very little about where the impetus for this change came from or what the reaction of regular Republicans to it was. Evidence from several northern states like Illinois, Ohio, Massachusetts, and California, however, suggests that some Republicans resented even changing the party's name. Many more vehemently opposed the steps Lincoln took to give that change real substance—sharing offices with Democrats and Unionists and trying to scuttle the antisouthern policies congressional Republicans demanded.[18]

There is, alas, no "smoking gun" in the form of a letter in which Lincoln explains his purpose or urges state Republican politicians to start Union organizations. Therefore one cannot prove that Lincoln initiated the creation of Union parties which began to appear in the North in the fall of 1861. Nevertheless, one can infer Lincoln's intentions from his behavior, especially when that behavior is correlated chronologically with efforts to start Union parties and help them win elections in various states. Specifically, his attempt to build a new bisectional Union party can be seen in his dispensation of federal patronage, his use of the presidential pulpit to define the purpose of the war as restoration of the Union rather than abolition or social revolution in the South, and his attempts to shape wartime policies toward the South, toward slavery, and toward blacks.

Contrary to the McKitrick thesis, for example, building the Union party rather than balancing factions within the existing Republican party determined Lincoln's cabinet selections throughout his presidency. For the most important post, secretary of state, he chose Seward who, he had been warned, favored the "abandonment" of the Republican party and "the early formation of new combinations, under the name of a 'Union party,' or something of that kind." No Republican, indeed, had been more sympathetic than Seward to the Union party movement in the upper South during the secession crisis, and no Republican knew so well what was needed to gain the Union party's support for the Lincoln administration. Thus the purpose of Seward's notorious memorandum to Lincoln (April 1, 1861) was contained in its emphatic insistence that "we must *Change the question before the Public from one upon Slavery, or about Slavery* for a question upon *Union* or *Disunion*." Although Lincoln disregarded the accompanying advice in this note to start a foreign war and to abandon Fort Sumter to prevent a collision with the Confederacy, he was in perfect agreement with Seward about changing the issue from slavery to union. Indeed, Seward remained Lincoln's primary coadjutor in the Union party scheme throughout the war. Hence it is no coincidence that at precisely the time in September 1862 that Gideon Welles was complaining in his diary that Seward was always closeted with Lincoln, "inculcating his political party notions," Salmon P. Chase was protesting in *his* diary that Lincoln "has already separated himself from the great body of the party which elected him." Nor is it a coincidence that Seward was the chief target in the cabinet of angry congressional Republicans. They knew that Seward's and Lincoln's hopes of a bisectional Union party directly conflicted with their own hope of preserving the Republicans as an exclusively northern and vigorously antisouthern, anti-Democratic organization.[19]

Lincoln also expected that his appointees as secretary of war would further the development of the new party, if only by attracting northern Democrats to it. One of the things that finally persuaded Lincoln to appoint the unsavory Simon Cameron was that he had been assured that "there are thousands of influential democrats in Pennsylvania, who would feel disposed to sustain an administration, of which he should be a member." Cameron lost his value as a lure to Democratic defectors, however, when he endorsed the recruitment of black troops in December 1861. So Lincoln exiled Cameron about as far away from negrophobic northern Democrats as he could—to Russia—and replaced him with another Pennsylvania Democrat, Edwin Stanton. Unlike Cameron, indeed, Stanton had never joined the Republican party, and he had even served briefly in Buchanan's cabinet. Thus an Ohioan gushed to the new secretary, "The great democracy of the West feel especially grateful that the administration has at last called into its councils so thorough and pure a Democrat as Edwin M. Stanton." That gratitude, Lincoln hoped, would be translated into Union votes in upcoming northern elections.[20]

Lincoln's selections from the border states even more clearly illustrate his intentions to replace the Republican party. The tiny Republican organizations there denounced Bell supporters and former Know-Nothings as "our enemies" and demanded posts in the cabinet for pure antislavery Republicans such as the Kentucky abolitionist Cassius M. Clay or Judge William Marshall of Maryland. Maryland Republicans specifically warned Lincoln that the appointment of Montgomery Blair would destroy the Republican organization in that state because Blair favored "a *de*-republicanizing of the party, and a coalition administration," "a sort of 'Union' party to take the place of the Republicans." Precisely because Lincoln sought the same kind of party reorganization, he ignored the pleas of Republicans and selected Blair as well as Edward Bates, another favorite of the proslavery conservatives who were the political enemies of border-state Republicans. For the same reason, despite the anguished protests of Republicans, he divided the lesser federal posts in the border states among Republicans, Bell men, and Democrats who supported the new Union parties.[21]

As the war dragged on, both Bates and Blair, like Seward, drew fire from angry congressional Republicans for delaying the harsh antisouthern, antislavery measures they demanded. Thus Lincoln's decision to replace both men in 1864 is usually interpreted as a concession to radical elements in the Republican party, an attempt to balance the dismissal of the radical Chase from the cabinet or a quid pro quo for John C. Frémont's withdrawal as an independent radical Republican candidate from the presidential campaign that year. Yet equally important in shaping Lincoln's decision was his awareness that the Union parties in both Missouri and Maryland had undergone fundamental transformations. By 1864 radical elements committed to immediate, uncompensated emancipation and the use of black troops had taken them over. Hence conservatives like Bates and Blair no longer served as adequate bridges to the Union parties whose support Lincoln sought. For him to retain their backing, Blair and Bates had to go.[22]

Lincoln also manipulated other federal appointments to build the Union party, especially in 1861 and 1862 when his attention was focused primarily on the North and the border states. It is true that outside of the border states the vast majority of civilian positions went to regular Republicans recommended by Republican congressmen. Nonetheless, Lincoln carefully placed Democrats in highly visible posts in order to woo Democratic backing for new Union organizations in the North. Not only the fact but the timing of these appointments reveals his purpose. The most conspicuous examples were the military commands he showered on Democratic favorites like John McClernand, Don Carlos Buell, and George B. McClellan, appointments that Seward heartily favored and that congressional Republicans increasingly denounced by 1862. Despite this growing protest, Lincoln retained them in command as long as they might lure Democratic votes to the Union parties in northern states—and only that long. Buell was dismissed on October 24, 1862, after the October congressional elections in Illinois, Indiana, Ohio, and Pennsylvania. McClellan received the axe on November 5, 1862, the day after elections in New York and New Jersey.[23]

Lincoln also attempted to attract Democrats to influential civilian or quasi-civilian positions at times when he hoped to advance the building of Union parties in particular states. The Union party held its organizing conventions in Indiana in June 1862 and in Illinois in September 1862, for example. On July 31, 1862, Lincoln asked the widely popular former Democratic governor of Indiana, Joseph Wright, to run as a Union candidate for Congress to help bring Democrats to the new organization. Failing in that endeavor, he appointed the Kentucky Democrat Joseph Holt to the new post of judge advocate general of the army on September 3. Holt was a great favorite among Indiana and Illinois Democrats who had boomed him as a Democratic presidential possibility in January 1862. Holt, of course, was also a prominent leader of Kentucky's Union party which, in a special session of the Kentucky legislature in August 1862, had spurned Lincoln's offer of compensation and denounced as intolerable the antislavery actions of Republicans in Congress. Thus Lincoln with a single stroke tried to pacify the Union party in Kentucky and to persuade Democrats to join it in Indiana and Illinois.[24]

One final example must suffice. Since 1860 California's Republican party had clung to power only because the Democrats were divided into pro-Union and prosouthern wings. In 1862 the leader of the Union Democrats, John Conness, approached the Republicans about merging the two organizations in a Union party, a merger that reached fruition in the state legislative session that began in January 1863 when Conness, to the dismay of many original Republicans, was elected to the United States Senate. Conness's chief ally as leader of the Union Democrats was Stephen J. Field. Hence when Lincoln nominated Field as a Supreme Court justice and circuit judge for California in late February 1863, he not only nurtured the new Union coalition emerging in California but he dramatically gave his blessing to the prominent role of Democrats in it, a prominence resented by most California Republicans.[25]

A closer look at the chronology of conventions and elections involving the Union party in the North and border states also helps explain Lincoln's attempts to delay or frustrate congressional and military initiatives toward abolition and the arming of blacks. One reason for Lincoln's cautious movement on these matters surely was his concern about keeping proslavery Southerners and negrophobic northern Democrats behind the war effort. Arming blacks, he declared in August 1862, could "turn 50,000 bayonets from the loyal Border States against us that were for us."[26] Yet Lincoln was equally worried about turning ballots against his cherished Union party.

Take, for example, his rapid reaction to Frémont's emancipation decree of August 30, 1861. That edict not only menaced Kentucky's future loyalty to the Union, but it also could, in the words of Kentucky's James Speed, "crush out every vistage [sic] of a union party in the state." Although the Kentucky Union party had already won congressional elections in June and the state's legislative elections in August, before Frémont's actions, the legislature itself was due to meet on September 2. More important, state conventions to organize Union parties that would combine Democrats and Republicans were scheduled to meet in September in both Ohio and New York, conventions that could easily fizzle unless Frémont were rebuked. Thus Lincoln requested Frémont to revoke his order on September 2 and commanded him to on September 11, much to the displeasure of congressional Republicans. Nor was it coincidental that Lincoln first sent the orders to remove Frémont from command on October 24, orders that were finally implemented on November 2. Though firing Frémont angered Republicans, it helped the broad-based Union parties score decisive triumphs in New York and Maryland on November 6.[27]

Lincoln's public revocation of General David Hunter's emancipation decree on May 19, 1862, must also be understood in terms of the political calendar. State conventions to launch the Union party were scheduled in Indiana on June 24, Pennsylvania and New Jersey on July 17, and Illinois on September 24. In addition, Ohio's Union party which had elected Democrat David Tod governor in 1861 was due to hold another state convention on August 21, 1862. Lincoln had to revoke Hunter's order, lest potential Democratic supporters for these parties be frightened away. For the same reason he made a point of publicizing his rejection of an offer of two Negro regiments from Indiana on August 4, his advice to a delegation of free blacks on August 14 that colonization was the best solution to the country's racial problem, and his famous reply to Horace Greeley on August 22 that restoration of the Union, not abolition, remained his primary goal. For Lincoln, of course, building a successful bisectional Union party was integral to restoring the Union. And his disavowal of any intention to emancipate the slaves or arm blacks was clearly meant to help build that party.[28]

It's true that Lincoln seemed to contradict these efforts to reassure negrophobic northern Democrats and proslavery border-state Union men when he issued his preliminary Emancipation Proclamation on September 22. But he tried to make even that palatable to the groups he was wooing. For one thing, the emancipation provisions of Congress's confiscation act of July 17 theoretically went into effect in September, so Lincoln's postponement of emancipation until January 1, 1863, seemed to delay actual implementation of abolition by government forces until after the fall elections of 1862.[29] Moreover, by exempting loyal slave states and indicating that Confederate states that returned to the Union before that date would escape abolition, he made it clear that he viewed emancipation as an effort to hasten the restoration of the Union, not to punish Southerners. Thus the measure was compatible with his insistence the previous December that "the integrity of the Union" was "the primary object of the contest" and that he wanted to prevent the war from degenerating "into a violent and remorseless revolutionary struggle."[30]

Equally important, Lincoln took steps to balance whatever losses the proclamation might cost the Union parties in the North and border states by reducing the Democratic vote. On September 24, 1862, he suspended *habeas corpus* throughout the nation for the duration of the war and ordered the military arrest of "all persons . . . guilty of any disloyal practice." Almost by definition such persons would not be supporters of the Union party; instead they would be potential voters against it. Thus the thousands of arrests made in 1862, 1863, and 1864, often immediately before elections took place, kept foes of the Union parties away from the polls.[31]

None of Lincoln's efforts, however, prevented a stunning Democratic comeback in the elections of 1862 in New York, New Jersey, Pennsylvania, Ohio, Indiana, and Illinois. The divergent responses of Lincoln and congressional Republicans to this Democratic resurgence illustrate well how their contrasting political strategies led to conflict between the two branches. Both correctly recognized that the Republicans or Union party had lost primarily because they had suffered significantly more drop-off in their vote since 1860 than the Democrats, but they differed in their explanation of that erosion. Lincoln attributed it to the absence of potential Union voters in the army. Most Republicans instead blamed it on abstention by disgusted Northerners who wanted much harsher policies toward the South and slavery, the kinds of policies Republicans thought Lincoln had thwarted. Congressional Republicans, in other words, believed that former Republican voters had abandoned the party when it in turn seemed to abandon its antisouthern platform.[32]

Equally revealing, angry Republicans bluntly pointed to Lincoln's attempt to include Democrats and Southerners in a new Union party as the chief cause of the debacle. "The Republican organization was voluntarily abandoned by the president and his leading followers, and a no-party Union was formed," fumed Ohio Senator John Sherman. If the Republicans "have the wisdom to throw overboard the old debris that joined them in the Union movement, they will succeed. If not, they are doomed." "Fear of offending the Democracy has been at the bottom of all our disasters," echoed Maine's William Pitt Fessenden. Chicago's Republican editor Joseph Medill also castigated Lincoln's courtship of Democrats. "It is enough to make the strongest men weep tears of blood. The President has allowed the Democratic party to shape the policy of the war and furnish the Generals to conduct it, while the Republicans have furnished the men and the money." What galled these Republicans, it bears repeating, was not simply sharing leadership positions with Democrats and border state Unionists. It was that courting such men precluded or at least obfuscated the punitive actions against the Slave Power like confiscation, abolition, and the arming of former slaves that Republicans thought their constituents wanted. By watering down the Republicans' antisouthern principles in favor of the diluted Union platform, Ohio's Joshua Giddings complained, Lincoln had condemned Republican candidates to enter the elections "without doctrines, principles, or character." The Democratic comeback of 1862, in sum, reinforced the conviction among congressional Republicans that they could defeat Democrats in the North only by retaining the Republican party's exclusively northern, antisouthern, anti-Democratic identity.[33]

That hardening of Republican opposition to the Union party strategy made further clashes with Lincoln inevitable, for the president viewed the Democratic comeback in the North as an even greater reason to press ahead with his plans before the 1864 presidential contest. The palpable failure of substantial numbers of northern Democrats to join the Union coalition probably made them less important in his calculations after 1862. We know he sacked Buell and McClellan immediately after the elections ended, and in January 1863 he went ahead with emancipation and the concomitant enrollment of black troops, policies he had tried to delay earlier. It's also clear that in 1863 and 1864 he relied less on inducements to Democrats than on the soldier vote he thought had been absent in 1862 to carry northern elections. On the other hand, after the 1862 debacle, he sought frantically to shore up Union organizations in the border states and to build them in the Confederate states in order to offset the renewed strength of the Democracy in the North with new support for himself in the South.[34]

By 1863 and 1864 Union parties had been successfully established in the border states. Moreover, they were increasingly falling under the lead of more radical men, at least in Missouri and Maryland, men who wanted to abolish slavery and ruthlessly proscribe their political enemies from voting. In the border states as in the North, therefore, Lincoln shifted course from seeking support for the Union parties to trying to weaken the Democratic challenge to them. He increased arrests of supposed Confederate sympathizers at election times and dispatched troops to guard the polls, troops that, not incidentally, intimidated potential Democratic voters. As a result, Democratic turnout in the border states in 1863 and 1864 dropped substantially from its 1860 levels. In this regard it is quite significant that Lincoln's amnesty proclamation of December 1863, however magnanimous it was toward Confederate states, specifically excluded the border states and the North from its provisions. Lincoln had no intention of restoring the vote to the most determined foes of the Union party in those states, especially since presidential amnesty would have overturned the draconian laws disfranchising Confederate sympathizers that state Union parties themselves had passed.[35]

Congressional Republicans readily approved Lincoln's new policies in the border states since they embodied the hard-nosed course they had long advocated. Furthermore, by 1863 and 1864 those Union parties and even the incipient Union organizations in Louisiana, Tennessee, and Arkansas were moving toward emancipation on their own. By 1864, in sum, the goal, if not the precise method, of abolition had ceased to be a bone of contention between Lincoln and Republican congressmen, and Lincoln happily endorsed the Thirteenth Amendment in the 1864 Union platform now that southern Union organizations accepted the inevitable end of slavery. The restoration of political rights and congressional representation to Confederate states and the inclusion of former Confederates in the Union party, however, were another matter. Here Lincoln and the congressional wing of his party remained at odds.

Almost as soon as the 1862 returns came in from the North, Lincoln bombarded his military governors in the occupied South with instructions to hold congressional elections, but Republicans in Congress refused to seat the few men who were chosen.[36] These Republicans were even more upset by the lenient terms of Lincoln's amnesty proclamation and ten percent plan, which, with the exception of a small group of Confederate civilian and military officials, restored political and property rights to those who took an oath of future allegiance and encouraged such men to establish and control civil governments that would replace the military regimes in their states. In contrast, congressional Republicans regarded former Confederates as traitors who did not deserve to vote, hold office, or be represented in Congress.

Lincoln's reconstruction policy of December 1863 was in fact a classic example of his attempt to find a middle road for his new Union party between the positions staked out by Democrats and congressional Republicans. Because Lincoln required Confederates who sought amnesty to swear that they and their new state governments would abide by his Emancipation Proclamation, Democrats who objected to any conditions being imposed on southern states as a price of restoration denounced the plan as too harsh. Besides, Democrats regarded the ten percent provisions as evidence that Lincoln was creating rotten boroughs to support him in 1864. Republicans, on the other hand, regarded the plan as far too lenient toward the Slave Power and therefore inimical to their attempt to run on an antisouthern platform in the North. For one thing, they wanted to require Confederate states to revise their constitutions to abolish slavery *before* they elected new state governments and sought readmission. Lincoln said nothing about this requirement in his proclamation, and he seemed prepared to ignore it when he allowed the Union party in Louisiana to elect new state officials in early 1864 before holding a constitutional convention. The difference was one of substance and not just procedure, for the area of Louisiana and Tennessee where Lincoln first tried to apply his policy had been exempted from emancipation by his proclamation. Lincoln's policy, in short, seemed far less certain than their own plan to eradicate slavery permanently, at least until the Thirteenth Amendment passed Congress and was ratified by the states. In addition, congressional Republicans wanted to force southern states to repudiate the Confederate debt as a price of readmission, a matter on which Lincoln's plan was silent. Finally, they wanted to limit the period during which Confederates could apply for pardon and to exclude many more former Confederates from the political process than Lincoln's plan seemed to.

For all these reasons, Republicans in July 1864 passed the more stringent Wade-Davis bill as a congressional alternative to Lincoln's plan of reconstruction.

While genuine differences of opinion over the proper policy as well as a jurisdictional conflict over control of reconstruction separated Lincoln from congressional Republicans, their contrasting political strategies also divided them. Lincoln clearly hoped to restore Confederate states to the Union as rapidly as possible, not only because he wanted their votes in 1864 but also because he wanted to prevent Congress from imposing radical changes on the South that might alienate white Southerners from the Union party. Congressional Republicans, in contrast, believed that Lincoln's efforts to lure such men to the Union party through generous policies repeated the mistake of 1862 that had produced Democratic victories in the North. As Herman Belz had ably demonstrated, congressional Republicans wanted to go before the northern electorate in 1864 with a concrete antislavery, antisouthern record. Thus, when the Thirteenth Amendment failed to pass Congress that year, they frantically framed the Wade-Davis bill and begged Lincoln to sign it so they could trumpet their anti–Slave Power credentials to their constituents. Yet precisely because the bill would postpone indefinitely the return of Confederate states to political participation and drive Southerners from the Union party Lincoln had worked so hard to build, he vetoed it. That veto, in turn, provoked a storm of protest from Republican leaders in Congress who refused to count the electoral votes cast by those Union parties in 1864 or to admit their chosen representatives to Congress after the election.

Perhaps no document reveals so plainly the differences between Lincoln and congressional Republicans, indeed, as does the extraordinary Wade-Davis Manifesto of August 1864 in which the Republican leadership spelled out for the northern public why the congressional plan was superior to the president's. Their own bill "exacted" as the price of readmission the "exclusion of dangerous enemies from power and the relief of the nation from the rebel debt, and the prohibition of slavery forever." In contrast, "the President is resolved that people shall not *by law* take *any* securities from the rebel States against a renewal of the rebellion, before restoring their power to govern us." Furious that Lincoln's veto and his own policy would undercut their preferred campaign strategy, congressional Republicans thus publicly repudiated the plan of their presidential candidate in order to reaffirm their own anti-southern credentials with the northern electorate.[37]

At the time of his death, therefore, Lincoln and congressional Republicans remained stalemated over reconstruction and the desirability of including former Confederates in a bisectional Union party. Still, one might argue that Lincoln achieved considerable success with his efforts at partisan reorganization. Despite considerable antagonism from congressional Republicans to his renomination in 1864, the state Union organizations he had worked so hard to nurture in the North, the border states, and the occupied South supported him, and he easily won renomination. Moreover, he engineered the dumping of Hannibal Hamlin and the selection of the Tennessee Democrat Andrew Johnson as his running mate on a ticket that carried the label of the National Union, not the Republican, party. Clearly Lincoln intended the substitution of Johnson for Hamlin as a signal that the Union party was both bipartisan and bisectional.[38] Finally, and most important, Lincoln received about 340,000 more votes in 1864 than in 1860, and about 146,000 of these new votes came from border states, where he actually carried Maryland, Missouri, and West Virginia. Here indeed was evidence that the party had extended its base to the South.

Yet it would be a profound mistake to conclude that Lincoln succeeded in transforming the Republican party into a genuine bisectional Union party dedicated to reunion rather than the humbling of white Southerners. For one thing, there is little evidence outside California of a substantial swing of northern Democrats to the Union party. Those northern Democrats who permanently joined the party, moreover, were men like John A. Logan of Illinois, later a famous waver of the Bloody Shirt and Stalwart supporter of Ulysses Grant. Most Democrats who joined the Union party during the war, just like most young soldiers who cast their first presidential ballot for Lincoln in 1864, were motivated primarily by hatred of the South engendered by the war itself, not by the spirit of sectional reconciliation Lincoln hoped to foster through the new party. Instead of changing or mitigating the anti-southern thrust of the Republican party, indeed, the Civil War only increased it by reinforcing the bitterness of Northerners toward their southern enemies. Thus in the years immediately following the war, congressional Republicans would strive to make their reconstruction policies and their rhetoric the political equivalent of war against the South.[39]

Given this intensification of antisouthern sentiment in the North, Lincoln's hope of creating a permanent new anti-Democratic Union party that could incorporate white Southerners in its ranks was doomed. Whatever the reasons for men from the border and Confederate states joining the Union party, they were not antisouthern. Hence the interests of northern and southern opponents of the Democrats were as much at odds as they had been in 1860. The inevitable failure of the Union party became evident when Lincoln's successor, Johnson, who continued Lincoln's efforts to include northern Democrats and anti-Democratic white Southerners in a national Union party, broke with congressional Republicans in 1866. By the fall of that year, those congressmen were campaigning once again as Republicans in open hostility to Johnson's—and Lincoln's—Union party. By the end of 1866, therefore, all hope of substituting a bisectional Union party for the Republicans as the major anti-Democratic party in American political life was gone.

The purpose of this essay, however, has not been to focus on the success or failure of the Union party. Rather it has been to suggest that Lincoln's attempt to build a Union party in response to the Democratic challenge and the determination of congressional Republicans to take a different tack to defeat Democrats was the chief source of the disagreements between Lincoln and Congress during the war. Furthermore, one can argue that their very divisions helped the North win the war. For where Lincoln took the lead, as in the use of arbitrary arrests and military intervention to bulwark Union parties in the border states or of amnesty and the ten percent plan to extend them to the Confederate South, or where Congress took the lead, as in the push for emancipation and the arming of black troops or with the nationalistic legislation passed to remove power from Democratic jurisdictions, the central tendency was toward a stronger war effort or greater weakening of the South. Put differently, Lincoln in effect used a carrot to induce Southerners to renounce the Confederacy and join a Union party that was not based on unremitting hostility to them, as the prewar Republican party had been. Congressional Republicans, in contrast, wanted to use a stick to beat Southerners into submission and thus please their northern constituents. The combination of the carrot and the stick, I suggest, was more successful than either would have been alone.

NOTES

1 / Eric McKitrick, "Party Politics and the Union and Confederate War Efforts," in *The American Party Systems: Stages of Political Development,* ed. William N. Chambers and Walter Dean Burnham (New York: Oxford University Press, 1967), 117–51.

2 / The historiographical debate on this topic has been extensive. Among the more important titles are T. Harry Williams, *Lincoln and the Radicals* (Madison: University of Wisconsin Press, 1941); David Donald, "The Radicals and Lincoln," in *Lincoln Reconsidered: Essays on the Civil War Era* (New York: Vintage Books, 1961), 103–27; David Donald, "Devils Facing Zionwards" and T. Harry Williams, "Lincoln and the Radicals: An Essay in Civil War History and Historiography," in *Grant, Lee, Lincoln and the Radicals,* ed. Grady McWhiney (New York: Harper and Row, 1966), 72–177; Hans L. Trefousse, *The Radical Republicans: Lincoln's Vanguard for Racial Justice* (New York: Alfred A. Knopf, 1969); Herman Belz, *Reconstructing the Union: Theory and Policy During the Civil War* (Ithaca: Cornell University Press, 1969); Michael Les Benedict, *A Compromise of Principle: Congressional Republicans and Reconstruction, 1863–1869* (New York: W. W. Norton and Co., 1974); James A. Rawley, *The Politics of Union: Northern Politics during the Civil War* (Hinsdale, Ill.: Dryden Press, 1974); and LaWanda Cox, *Lincoln and Black Freedom: A Study in Presidential Leadership* (Columbia: University of South Carolina Press, 1981).

3 / My argument here in no way denies the importance of other factors that contributed to tensions between Lincoln and Congress such as jurisdictional conflicts between the executive and legislative branches or Congress's ideological opposition to Lincoln's reconstruction policies because they inadequately protected blacks or secured republican self-government. Rather, my point is that the different political strategies pursued by Lincoln and congressional Republicans was the chief source of the conflicts over policy between them. David Donald has briefly suggested a somewhat similar interpretation in *The Politics of Reconstruction, 1863–1867* (Baton Rouge: LSU Press, 1965), 11–17.

4 / For an elaboration of my understanding of Republican appeals in the 1850s, see Michael F. Holt, *The Political Crisis of the 1850s,* reprint ed. (New York: W. W. Norton and Co., 1983), 183–217

5 / *New York Tribune,* June 18, 1862, quoting Benjamin Wade and Congressman John T. Nixon, both quoted in Williams, *Lincoln and the Radicals,* 139, 159.

6 / These are primarily the Republican congressmen from New York City, Philadelphia, and California.

7 / J. H. Jordan to Lyman Trumbull, February 20, 1862, quoted in Williams, *Lincoln and the Radicals,* 11. Belz, *Reconstructing the Union,* provides extensive evidence that, except for a brief period in 1863, Lincoln and congressional Republicans disagreed about the manner of and conditions for restoring Confederate states to the Union from the summer of 1861 until the end of the war.

8 / David Donald, "Abraham Lincoln: Whig in the White House," in *Lincoln Reconsidered*, 187–208.

9 / *The Collected Works of Abraham Lincoln*, ed. Roy P. Basler, Marion Delores Pratt, and Lloyd A. Dunlap, 9 vols. (New Brunswick, N.J.: Rutgers University Press, 1953–55), 4:439.

10 / Lincoln to Johnson, July 3, 1862, and to John A. Dix, October 26, 1862, ibid., 5:302–3, 476. See also Belz, *Reconstructing the Union*, 105–10 and passim.

11 / Holt, *The Political Crisis of the 1850s*, 219–59; William J. Cooper, Jr., *The South and the Politics of Slavery, 1828–1856* (Baton Rouge: LSU Press, 1978), 341–74; and William J. Cooper, Jr., *Liberty and Slavery: Southern Politics to 1860* (New York: Alfred A. Knopf, 1983), 243–81.

12 / This point is forcefully argued in the two books by Cooper cited above.

13 / Francis Blackburn to Lincoln, Philadelphia, November 24, 1860, James K. Moorhead to Lincoln, Pittsburgh, November 23, 1860, Abraham Lincoln Papers, Library of Congress (microfilm edition). On the difference between the Republican party and the People's party in Pennsylvania and New Jersey, see also Michael Fitzgibbon Holt, *Forging a Majority: The Formation of the Republican Party in Pittsburgh, 1848–1860* (New Haven: Yale University Press, 1969), 264–69.

14 / The best study of the Union party movement in the upper South in Daniel W. Crofts, "The Union Party of 1861 and the Secession Crisis," *Perspectives in American History* 11 (1977–78): 327–76. For the embryonic realignment in the lower South, see Peyton McCrary, Clark Miller, and Dale Baum, "Class and Party in the Secession Crisis: Voting Behavior in the Deep South, 1856–1861," *Journal of Interdisciplinary History* 8 (1978): 429–57.

15 / Gilmer to Lincoln, December 29, 1860, Lincoln Papers; Gilmer to Weed, January 12, 1861, and *Richmond Whig*, February 13, 1861, quoted in Crofts, "The Union Party of 1861," 357.

16 / *New York Times*, February 26, 1861, quoted in Crofts, "The Union Party of 1861," 358; Henry J. Raymond to Lincoln, December 14, 1860; Thomas C. Jones to Lincoln, December 24, 1860; and John D. Defrees to Lincoln, December 15, 1860, Lincoln Papers.

17 / B. F. Diggs to George W. Julian, January 16, 1861, quoted in Williams, *Lincoln and the Radicals*, 15. For examples of letters warning Lincoln not to compromise, see C. F. Jack to Lincoln, December 5, 1860, and Carl Schurz to Lincoln, December 18, 1860, Lincoln Papers. Lincoln's correspondence prior to his inauguration was filled with such letters, but it also contained many urging him to make concessions to the South. The basic study of the hardening of Republican opinion against compromise with the South during the secession crisis is Kenneth M. Stampp, *And the War Came: The North and the Secession Crisis, 1860–61* (Baton Rouge: LSU Press, 1950).

18 / For examples of historians who consider the adoption of the Union name a facade, see James G. Randall, *Lincoln the President*, 4 vols. (New York: Dodd, Mead and Co., 1945–55), vol. 2, *Springfield to Gettysburg*, 214–16, and Joel H. Silbey, *A Respectable Minority: The Democratic Party in the Civil War Era, 1860–1868* (New York: W. W. Norton and Co., 1977), 40–61. We need much more systematic study of the reactions by congressional Republicans and state-level Republican politicians to the formation of Union coalitions in the North. I have not done that research myself and have gleaned information about the states mentioned from the following sources. For Illinois there is an excellent discussion of the origins of and reaction to the Union party movement in Gary Lee Cardwell, "The Rise of the Stalwarts and the Transformation of Illinois Repub-

lican Politics, 1860–1880" (Ph.D. diss., University of Virginia, 1976), 37–89, esp. 52–76. On Ohio, I have had an opportunity to read Frederick J. Blue's manuscript biography, "Salmon P. Chase: A Life in Politics," which suggests a negative reaction on p. 584, n. 57. For California I have relied on conversations with my colleague Professor Charles W. McCurdy, who is writing a biography of Stephen J. Field, one of the leaders in forming California's Union party. Finally, for Massachusetts where the Union or People's party formed explicitly as a conservative foe of the Republicans and of the re-election of Charles Sumner to the Senate, I used David Donald, *Charles Sumner and the Rights of Man* (New York: Alfred A. Knopf, 1970), 67–86. In addition to the specific examples included below in the text, Williams, *Lincoln and the Radicals,* is a compendium of Republican complaints about Lincoln's appointments and policies.

19 / George Fogg to Lincoln, February 5, 1861, quoted in Crofts, "The Union Party of 1861," 368 n. 48; Leonard Swett to Lincoln, December 31, 1860, and Seward to Lincoln, December 25, 1860, Lincoln Papers. Seward's April 1 memorandum is printed in *Collected Works of Lincoln,* 4:317. The Crofts article is the best account of Seward's attempt to build a Union party in 1860–61, but for his continuing efforts during the war see also LaWanda Cox and John H. Cox, *Politics, Principle, and Prejudice 1865–1866: Dilemma of Reconstruction America* (New York: The Free Press of Glencoe, 1963), 31–49.

The quotations from the cabinet diaries come from Welles's entry for September 16, 1862, and from Chase's entry for September 12, 1862. See Howard K. Beale, ed., *Diary of Gideon Welles,* 3 vols. (New York: W. W. Norton and Co., 1960), 1:136; and David Donald, ed., *Inside Lincoln's Cabinet: The Civil War Diaries of Salmon P. Chase* (New York: Longmans, Green and Co., 1954), 136.

20 / David Taggart to Lincoln, December 17, 1860, Lincoln Papers; A.G.W. Carter to Edwin M. Stanton, January 17, 1862, quoted in Williams, *Lincoln and the Radicals,* 91.

21 / Curtis Knight to George D. Blakey, Kingston, Ky., December 15, 1860; Joseph Calvert to Lincoln, Bowling Green, Ky., December 28, 1860; and W. G. Snethen to Lincoln, Baltimore, November 26, December 8, 13, 1860, Lincoln Papers. For Lincoln's other patronage appointments in the border states, see Harry J. Carman and Reinhard H. Luthin, *Lincoln and the Patronage,* reprint ed. (Gloucester, Mass.: Peter Smith, 1964), 186–227; and William B. Hesseltine, *Lincoln's Plan of Reconstruction* (Chicago: Quadrangle Books, 1967), 19–30.

22 / For these developments in the border states, see Jean H. Baker, *The Politics of Continuity: Maryland Political Parties from 1858 to 1870* (Baltimore: The Johns Hopkins University Press, 1973), 77–110; and William E. Parrish, *A History of Missouri* (Columbia: University of Missouri Press, 1973), vol. 3, *1860 to 1875,* 87–115.

23 / Williams, *Lincoln and the Radicals,* 190–95; Carman and Luthin, *Lincoln and the Patronage.*

24 / *Collected Works of Lincoln,* 5:351–52, 538 n.; Randall, *Lincoln the President,* 2:213; *Appleton's Annual Cyclopaedia for 1862,* 519, 527–28, 541.

25 / *Collected Works of Lincoln,* 6:113. Again, I have relied primarily on my colleague Professor Charles W. McCurdy for information on the political situation in California.

26 / "Remarks to Deputation of Western Gentlemen," August 4, 1862, in *Collected Works of Lincoln,* 5:356–57.

27 / Speed to Lincoln, September 3, 1861, ibid., 4:506–7 n.; Lincoln's actions can be followed in ibid., 506–7, 517–18, 562–63. Dates for convention meetings and elections were taken from *Appleton's Annual Cyclopaedia for 1861* and the *Tribune Almanac.* See also Silbey, *A Respectable Minority,* 39–42.

28 / Dates for convention meetings are given under the entries for the respective

states in *Appleton's Annual Cyclopaedia for 1862*. Lincoln's statements and orders can be found in *Collected Works of Lincoln*, vol. 5, for the dates indicated.

29 / David Donald makes this point in *Charles Sumner and the Rights of Man*, 81.

30 / *Collected Works of Lincoln*, 5:49.

31 / Ibid., 5:436–37. A number of historians have commented on the calculated reduction of the Democratic vote in the North and border states through the use of arbitrary arrests and military intervention. See, for example, Hesseltine, *Lincoln's Plan of Reconstruction*, 31–47 and passim. Forceful suppression of the Democratic vote also forms a central theme of William B. Hesseltine, *Lincoln and the War Governors* (New York: Alfred A. Knopf, 1948).

32 / See, for example, the revealing exchange between Lincoln and Carl Schurz about the reasons for the Republican or Union defeats in *Collected Works of Lincoln*, 5:493–95, 509–11. On the dramatic difference between the size of Democratic and Republican drop-off in 1862, see table 3.4 in Paul Kleppner, *The Third Electoral System, 1853–1892: Parties, Voters, and Political Cultures* (Chapel Hill: University of North Carolina Press, 1979), 77.

33 / John Sherman to William T. Sherman, November 16, 1862; William Pitt Fessenden to John Murray Forbes, November 13, 1862; Joseph Medill to Lyman Trumbull, November 14, 1862; and Joshua Giddings to George W. Julian, March 22, 1863, all quoted in Williams, *Lincoln and the Radicals*, 15, 188–90. Note that it was immediately after these defeats in the fall of 1862 that Senate Republicans tried to purge Seward and that Congress passed nationalistic legislation aimed at stripping state governments of their jurisdiction over banking, manpower, and legal proceedings against federal military and civilian officials.

34 / Belz, *Reconstructing the Union*, 109–10, also recognizes that Lincoln pressed ahead with his party-building efforts in the South in order to offset Democratic gains in the North.

35 / In addition to the books on Maryland and Missouri by Baker and Parrish cited earlier, see the discussion of the wartime political experience of the different border states in the essays in Richard O. Curry, ed., *Radicalism, Racism, and Party Realignment: The Border States during Reconstruction* (Baltimore: The Johns Hopkins University Press, 1969).

36 / Five congressmen elected from occupied areas of the Confederacy sought to be seated when Congress met in December 1862. The House refused to seat three from Virginia, North Carolina, and Tennessee. On the other hand, it did admit the two men elected from Louisiana, but only in late February 1863, a few days before the Thirty-Seventh Congress permanently adjourned in early March. See Belz, *Reconstructing the Union*, 110–15.

37 / The Wade-Davis Manifesto is quoted in ibid., 229, 242–43. I have relied primarily on Belz, 168–243, for this analysis of the split between Lincoln and Congress over reconstruction in 1864. Other recent accounts that explore the Wade-Davis bill in detail and that also stress the crucial role of developments in Louisiana are: Benedict, *A Compromise of Principle*, 70–99; Cox, *Lincoln and Black Freedom*, 46–139; and Peyton McCrary, *Abraham Lincoln and Reconstruction: The Louisiana Experiment* (Princeton: Princeton University Press, 1978).

38 / The best discussion of the maneuvering behind Johnson's nomination is James G. Randall and Richard Current, *Lincoln the President: Last Full Measure* (New York: Dodd, Mead and Co., 1955), 130–34.

39 / The constancy of Democratic voting support during the war is a central theme of Silbey, *A Respectable Minority*. The extent to which hatred of the South motivated the Democrats who joined the Illinois Union party during the war and remained in the

Republican party after the war is a central theme of Gary Cardwell's dissertation, "The Rise of the Stalwarts and the Transformation of Illinois Republican Politics, 1860–1880." Studies of the motivations of Democrats who joined the Union party in other northern states would be most welcome.

JAMES M. MCPHERSON

★

Abraham Lincoln and
the Second American Revolution

THE FOREMOST LINCOLN SCHOLAR OF A GENERATION AGO,
James G. Randall, considered the sixteenth president to be a conservative on the great issues facing the country, Union and slavery. If conservatism, wrote Randall, meant "caution, prudent adherence to tested
values, avoidance of rashness, and reliance upon unhurried, peaceable
evolution, [then] Lincoln was a conservative." His preferred solution of
the slavery problem, Randall pointed out, was a program of gradual,
compensated emancipation with the consent of the owners, stretching
over a generation or more, with provision for the colonization abroad
of emancipated slaves to minimize the potential for racial conflict and
social disorder. In his own words, Lincoln said that he wanted to "stand
on middle ground," avoid "dangerous extremes," and achieve his goals
through "the spirit of compromise . . . [and] of mutual concession."
In essence, concluded Randall, Lincoln believed in *evolution* rather than
revolution, in "planting, cultivating, and harvesting, not in uprooting
and destroying."[1] Many historians have agreed with this interpretation. To cite just two of them: T. Harry Williams maintained that
"Lincoln was on the slavery question, as he was on most matters, a conservative"; and Norman Graebner wrote an essay entitled "Abraham
Lincoln: Conservative Statesman," based on the premise that Lincoln

was a conservative because "he accepted the need of dealing with things as they were, not as he would have wished them to be."[2]

Yet as president of the United States, Lincoln presided over what Georges Clemenceau, future premier of France, described as "one of the most radical revolutions known in history," the destruction of slavery and the old South. Another future prime minister, Benjamin Disraeli of Britain, in 1863 characterized "the struggle in America" as "a great revolution. . . . [We] will see, when the waters have subsided, a different America."[3] The *Springfield Republican,* a prominent northern newspaper, predicted in 1862 that the Emancipation Proclamation would accomplish "the greatest social and political revolution of the age." The historian Otto Olsen has labeled Lincoln a revolutionary because he led the nation in its accomplishment of this result.[4] As for Lincoln himself, he said repeatedly that the right of revolution, the "right of any people" to "throw off, to revolutionize, their existing form of government, and to establish such other in its stead as they may choose" was "a sacred right—a right, which we may hope and believe, is to liberate the world." The American Declaration of Independence, he insisted often, was the great "charter of freedom" and in the example of the American Revolution "the world has found . . . the germ . . . to grow and expand into the universal liberty of mankind." Lincoln had championed the leaders of the European revolutions of 1848; in turn, a man who knew something about those revolutions and about revolution in general—Karl Marx—praised Lincoln in 1865 as "the single-minded son of the working class" who had led his "country through a matchless struggle . . . [a] world-transforming . . . revolutionary movement . . . for the rescue of an enchained race and the reconstruction of a social world."[5]

What are we to make of these contrasting portraits of Lincoln the conservative and Lincoln the revolutionary? Is this just another example of how Lincoln's words can be manipulated to support any position, even diametrically opposed ones? Or is it a problem of interpretation and emphasis within the context of a fluid and rapidly changing crisis situation, the American Civil War, which started out as one sort of conflict and ended as something quite different? I think it is the latter; therefore I think that these apparently contradictory positions about Lincoln the conservative versus Lincoln the revolutionary can be reconciled. And the attempt to reconcile them can tell us a great deal about the nature of the American Civil War.

THAT WAR has been viewed as a revolution—as the second American Revolution—in three different senses. Lincoln played a crucial role in defining the outcome of the revolution in each of these three respects.

The first way in which some contemporaries regarded the events of 1861 as a revolution was the South's invocation of the right of revolution to justify their secession—their declaration of independence—from the United States. The Mississippi convention that voted to secede in 1861 listed all the state's grievances against the North, and added: "For far less cause than this, our fathers separated from the Crown of England." The governor of Tennessee agreed that unless the North made concessions to the South, "the only alternative left to us [will be] to follow the example of our fathers of 1776." And an Alabama newspaper asked rhetorically: Were not "the men of 1776, who withdrew their allegiance from George III and set up for themselves . . . Secessionists?"[6]

Southerners created the Confederacy to protect what they called their "liberty" against a perceived northern threat to that liberty. Just as the Declaration of Independence had proclaimed the right of a people to alter or abolish their form of government when it threatened life, liberty, and pursuit of happiness, so southern declarations of secession proclaimed their right to alter the oppressive form of government that the inauguration of a Republican president in Washington would impose on them. "I took up arms," declared a Confederate officer in the middle of the war, upon the ground of "the right of revolution. Our properties and liberties were about to be taken from us. It was a sacred duty to rebel."[7]

There was a tragic irony in this southern justification of secession as a revolution to preserve liberty. The chief liberty they feared threatened by Lincoln's election was their right to own slaves and to take them where they pleased in territories of the United States. Most southern whites believed that their own liberty required the slavery of black people. The preeminent advocate of secession, William Lowndes Yancey of Alabama, put it this way: "Your fathers and my fathers [i.e., the men of the Revolution] built this government on two ideas. The first is that the white race is the citizen, and the master race, and the white man is the equal of every other white man. The second idea is that the negro is the inferior race." In this interpretation of the Declaration of Independence, it was only *white* men who were created equal. In the southern social structure, racial caste replaced class as the principal social demarcation. As John C. Calhoun explained: "With us, the two great divisions of society are not the rich and the poor, but white and black; and all the former, the poor as well as the rich, belong to the upper class, and are respected and treated as equals."[8]

It was this white equality based on black slavery that constituted the main liberty the South believed jeopardized by Lincoln's election. After all, they pointed out, the president-elect had said two years earlier in his House Divided speech that the country could not survive forever half slave and half free. The Republicans, Lincoln had stated, believed that it must become all free, and their program for excluding slavery from the territories was the first step in that direction. No matter that Lincoln and the Republican party promised not to interfere with slavery in the states where it already existed. The ideology and thrust of the "Black Republicans," as Southerners called them, were antislavery, and Lincoln's election to the presidency was the handwriting on the wall that doomed southern liberties if the South remained in the Union. A Georgia secessionist declared rather hysterically in 1860 that if the South did not secede from a "government ruled by Lincoln and his crew . . . in TEN years or less our children will be the *slaves* of negroes. For emancipation must follow and negro equality is the same result."[9]

The irony of this revolution in behalf of liberty to preserve slavery did not escape northern Republicans, including Lincoln. The *New York Tribune* pointed out that "Mr. Jefferson's Declaration of Independence was made in the interest of natural rights against Established Institutions. Mr. Jeff[erson] Davis's caricature thereof is made in the interest of an unjust, outgrown, decaying Institution against the apprehended encroachments of Natural Human Rights." Lincoln noted that "we all declare for liberty; but in using the same *word* we do not all mean the same thing." For Northerners "liberty" meant "for each man to do as he pleases with himself, and the product of his labor," said Lincoln, while for Southerners "the same word may mean for some men to do as they please with other men, and the product of other men's labor." In December 1860 Lincoln wrote to his old friend Alexander Stephens (who subsequently became vice president of the Confederacy) that although the Lincoln administration would never interfere with the right of Southerners to continue owning their slaves in the South, "I suppose . . . this does not meet the case. You think slavery is *right* and ought to be extended; while we think it is *wrong* and ought to be restricted. That I suppose is the rub." It was indeed the rub.[10]

Northerners could scarcely deny to the South the right of revolution for just cause, since Yankees were as much heirs of the legacy of 1776 as Southerners were. But that phrase, "for just cause," is crucial. As Lincoln himself put it in the summer of 1861, "the right of revolution, is never a legal right. . . . At most, it is but a moral right, when exercised for a morally justifiable cause. When exercised without such a cause revolution is no right, but simply a wicked exercise of physical power."[11] Secession was just such a wicked exercise. The event that precipitated it was Lincoln's election. Yet that election had been achieved by a constitutional majority according to constitutional procedures. The Republicans had done nothing against the law, had violated nobody's constitutional rights. Indeed, seven southern states had seceded and formed the Confederacy a month before Lincoln took office. In the view of Lincoln and of most Northerners, the South, having controlled the national government for most of the previous two generations through its domination of the Democratic party, now decided to leave the Union just because it had lost an election.

For Lincoln it was the *Union,* not the Confederacy, that was the true heir of the Revolution of 1776. That revolution had established a republic, a democratic government of the people by the people. This republic was a fragile experiment in a world of kings, emperors, tyrants, and theories of aristocracy. If secession were allowed to succeed, it would destroy that experiment. It would set a fatal precedent by which the minority could secede whenever it did not like what the majority stood for, until the United States fragmented into a dozen pitiful, squabbling countries, the laughing stock of the world. The successful establishment of a slaveholding Confederacy would also enshrine the idea of inequality, a contradiction of the ideal of equal natural rights on which the United States was founded. "The central idea of this struggle," said Lincoln during the war, "is the necessity . . . of proving that popular government is not an absurdity. We must settle this question now, whether in a free government the minority have the right to break up the government whenever they choose." "This issue embraces more than the fate of these United States," said Lincoln on another occasion. "It presents to the whole family of man, the question, whether a constitutional republic, or a democracy . . . can, or cannot, maintain its territorial integrity." Nor is the struggle "altogether for today; it is for a vast future. . . . On the side of the Union it is a struggle for maintaining in the world that form and substance of government whose leading object is to elevate the condition of men . . . to afford all an unfettered start, and a fair chance in the race of life."[12]

Thus with regard to the first sense in which many people viewed the Civil War as a revolution—a war of independence by the South—Lincoln denied the revolutionary legitimacy of the Confederacy and did more than any other person to defeat it. In this sense he was most certainly a conservative, for he worked to conserve the Union against the South's revolutionary attempt to overthrow it.

THE SECOND respect in which we can view the Civil War as a revolution was in its abolition of slavery. This was indeed a revolutionary achievement. As property, the four million slaves carried a value of some three billion dollars in 1860. This is difficult to translate into today's dollars, but as a proportion of total national wealth it would be equivalent to several hundred billion dollars today. It was equal to about two-thirds of the gross national product in 1860. In abolishing slavery during the Civil War, the government in effect confiscated the principal form of wealth in half of the country. It transferred the ownership of this human capital from the slaveowners to the former slaves themselves. When such a massive confiscation of wealth and transfer of capital from rich to poor takes place, we rightly call it a revolution. But of course owning slaves was more than a matter of owning property. It was basic to the southern social order, the political structure, the culture, the way of life in this region. Abolishing slavery amounted to a violent revolutionary destruction of this way of life.

From the beginning of the war, abolitionists and some Republicans urged the Lincoln administration to turn the military conflict into a revolutionary crusade to abolish slavery and create a new order in the South. As one abolitionist put it in 1861, although the Confederates "justify themselves under the right of revolution," their cause "is not a revolution but a rebellion against the noblest of revolutions." The North must meet this southern counterrevolution by converting the war for the Union into a revolution for freedom. *"We are the revolutionists,"* he proclaimed. The principal defect of the first American Revolution, in the eyes of abolitionists, had been that while it freed white Americans from British rule it failed to free black Americans from slavery. Now was the time to remedy that defect by proclaiming emancipation and inviting the slaves "to a share in the *glorious second American Revolution.*" And Thaddeus Stevens, the grim-visaged old congressman who led the radical Republicans in the House of Representatives, pulled no punches in this regard. "We must treat this [war] as a radical revolution," he declared, and "free every slave—slay every traitor— burn every rebel mansion, if these things be necessary to preserve" the nation.[13]

Such words grated harshly on Lincoln's ears during the first year of the war. In his message to Congress in December 1861 the president deplored the possibility that the war might "degenerate into a violent and remorseless revolutionary struggle." It was not that Lincoln *wanted* to preserve slavery. On the contrary, he said many times: "I am naturally anti-slavery. If slavery is not wrong, nothing is wrong." But as president he could not act officially on his private "judgment [concerning] the moral question of slavery." He was bound by the Constitution, which protected the institution of slavery in the states.[14] In the first year of the war the North fought to preserve this Constitution and restore the Union as it had existed before 1861. Lincoln's theory of the war held that since secession was illegal, the Confederate states were still legally in the Union although temporarily under the control of insurrectionists. The government's purpose was to suppress this insurrection and restore loyal Unionists to control of the southern states. The conflict was therefore a limited war, a "police action" if you will, with the limited goal of restoring the status quo ante bellum, not an unlimited war to destroy an enemy nation and reshape its society. And since, in theory, the southern states were still in the Union, they continued to enjoy all their constitutional rights, including slavery.

There were also a number of practical political reasons for Lincoln to take this conservative position in 1861. For one thing, the four border slave states of Missouri, Kentucky, Maryland, and Delaware had remained in the Union, and Lincoln desperately wanted to keep them there. He would like to have God on his side, Lincoln supposedly said, but he *must* have Kentucky. In all of these four states except Delaware a strong pro-Confederate faction existed. Any rash action by the northern government against slavery, therefore, might well push three more states into the Confederacy. Moreover, in the North itself nearly half the voters were Democrats, who supported a war for the Union but might oppose a war against slavery. For these reasons, Lincoln held at bay the Republicans and abolitionists who were calling for an antislavery war and revoked actions by two of his generals who had proclaimed emancipation by martial law in areas under their command.

Antislavery Republicans challenged the theory underlying Lincoln's concept of a limited war. They pointed out that by 1862 the conflict had become in theory as well as in fact a full-fledged war between nations, not just a police action to suppress an uprising. By imposing a blockade on Confederate ports and treating captured Confederate soldiers as prisoners of war rather than as criminals or pirates, the Lincoln administration had in effect recognized that this was a war rather than a mere domestic insurrection. Under international law, belligerent powers had the right to seize or destroy enemy resources used to wage war—munitions, ships, military equipment, even food for the armies and crops sold to obtain cash to buy armaments. As the war escalated in scale and fury and as Union armies invaded the South in 1862, they did destroy or capture such resources. Willy-nilly the war *was* becoming a remorseless revolutionary conflict, a total war rather than a limited one. A major Confederate resource for waging war was the slave population, which constituted a majority of the southern labor force. Slaves raised food for the army, worked in war industries, built fortifications, dug trenches, drove army supply wagons, and so on. As enemy property, these slaves were subject to confiscation under the laws of war. The Union Congress passed limited confiscation laws in August 1861 and July 1862 which authorized the seizure of this human property. But pressure mounted during 1862 to go further than this—to proclaim emancipation as a *means* of winning the war by converting the slaves from a vital war resource for the South to allies of the North, and beyond this to make the abolition of slavery a *goal* of the war, in order to destroy the institution that had caused the war in the first place and would continue to plague the nation in the future if it were allowed to survive. By the summer of 1862, most Republicans wanted to turn this limited war to restore the old Union into a revolutionary war to create a new nation purged of slavery.

Lincoln for a time tried to outflank this pressure by persuading the border slave states remaining in the Union to undertake voluntary, gradual emancipation, with the owners being compensated by the federal government. With rather dubious reasoning, Lincoln predicted that such action would shorten the war by depriving the Confederacy of its hope for the allegiance of these states and thereby induce the South to give up the fight. And though the compensation of slaveholders would be expensive, it would cost much less than continuing the war. If the border states adopted some plan of gradual emancipation such as northern states had done after the Revolution of 1776, said Lincoln, the process would not radically disrupt the social order.

Three times in the spring and summer of 1862 Lincoln appealed to congressmen from the border states to endorse a plan for gradual emancipation. If they did not, he warned in March, "it is impossible to foresee all the incidents which may attend and all the ruin which may follow." In May he declared that the changes produced by his gradual plan "would come gently as the dews of heaven, not rending or wrecking anything. Will you not embrace it? . . . You can not, if you would, be blind to the signs of the times." But the border-state representatives remained blind to the signs. They questioned the constitutionality of Lincoln's proposal, objected to its cost, bristled at its veiled threat of federal coercion, and deplored the potential race problem they feared would come with a large free black population. In July, Lincoln once more called border-state congressmen to the White House. He admonished them bluntly that "the unprecedentedly stern facts of the case" called for immediate action. The limited war was becoming a total war; pressure to turn it into a war of abolition was growing. If the border states did not make "a decision at once to emancipate *gradually* . . . the institution in your states will be extinguished by mere friction and abrasion—by the mere incidents of the war." In other words, if they did not accept an *ev*olutionary plan for the abolition of slavery, it would be wiped out by the revolution that was coming. But again they refused, voting by a margin of twenty to nine against Lincoln's proposal. Angry and disillusioned, the president decided to embrace the revolution. That very evening he made up his mind to issue an emancipation proclamation. After a delay to wait for a Union victory, he sent forth the preliminary proclamation on September 22, after the battle of Antietam, and the final proclamation on New Year's Day 1863.[15]

The old cliché, that the proclamation did not free a single slave be-cause it applied only to the Confederate states where Lincoln had no power, completely misses the point. The proclamation announced a revolutionary new war aim—the overthrow of slavery by force of arms if and when Union armies conquered the South. Of course, emancipa-tion could not be irrevocably accomplished without a constitutional amendment, so Lincoln threw his weight behind the Thirteenth Amendment, which was adopted in 1865. In the meantime two of the border states, Maryland and Missouri, which had refused to consider gradual, compensated emancipation in 1862, came under control of emancipationists who pushed through state constitutional amendments in 1864 that abolished slavery without compensation and went into effect immediately—a fate experienced by the other border states, Kentucky and Delaware, along with the rest of the South when the Thirteenth Amendment was ratified in 1865.

But from the time the Emancipation Proclamation went into effect at the beginning of 1863, the North fought for the revolutionary goal of a new Union without slavery. Despite grumbling and dissent by some soldiers, the Union army understood the new policy. A colonel from Indiana put it this way: "There is a desire [among my men] to destroy everything that [in any way] gives the rebels strength." Therefore "this army will sustain the emancipation proclamation and enforce it with the bayonet." Soon after the proclamation came out, General-in-Chief Henry W. Halleck wrote to General Ulysses Grant near Vicksburg that "the character of the war has very much changed within the last year. There is now no possible hope of reconciliation with the rebels. . . . We must conquer the rebels or be conquered by them. . . . Every slave withdrawn from the enemy is the equivalent of a white man put *hors de combat*." One of Grant's field commanders explained that "the policy is to be terrible on the enemy. I am using negroes all the time for my work as teamsters, and have 1,000 employed."[16]

Lincoln sanctioned this policy of "being terrible" on the enemy. And the policy soon went beyond using freed slaves as teamsters and labor-ers. By early 1863 the Lincoln administration committed itself to en-listing black men in the Union army. Arms in the hands of slaves constituted the South's ultimate nightmare. The enlistment of black soldiers to fight and kill their former masters was by far the most revo-lutionary dimension of the emancipation policy. And, after overcoming his initial hesitation, Lincoln became an enthusiastic advocate of this policy. In March 1863 he wrote to the military governor of occupied Tennessee: "The bare sight of fifty thousand armed, and drilled black soldiers on the banks of the Mississippi, would end the rebellion at once. And who doubts that we can present that sight, if we but take hold in earnest?" By August 1863, when the Union army had organized 50,000 black soldiers and was on its way to the enlistment of 180,000 before the war was over, Lincoln declared in a public letter that "the emancipation policy, and the use of colored troops, constitute the heaviest blow yet dealt to the rebellion."[17]

When conservatives complained of the revolutionary nature of these heavy blows, Lincoln responded that the nation could no longer pursue "a temporizing and forbearing" policy toward rebels. The government could not fight this war, said Lincoln sarcastically, "with elder-stalk squirts, charged with rose water." No, he continued, "decisive and extensive measures must be adopted." Conservatives who didn't like it should blame the southern slaveholders and fire-eaters who started the war. They "must understand," said Lincoln in an angry tone, "that they cannot experiment for ten years trying to destroy the government, and if they fail still come back into the Union unhurt." In a metaphor that he used repeatedly, Lincoln said that "broken eggs cannot be mended." The egg of slavery was already broken by 1862; if the South continued fighting it must expect more eggs to be broken, so the sooner it gave up "the smaller [would] be the amount of that which will be beyond mending."[18] Lincoln's fondness for this metaphor is interesting, for modern revolutionaries sometimes use a similar one to justify the use of violence to bring about social change: you cannot make an omelet, they say, without breaking eggs—that is, you cannot make a new society without destroying the old one.

Another way of illustrating how Lincoln came to believe in this revolutionary concept is to quote from his second inaugural address, when the war had gone on for almost four terrible years. I don't mean the famous words of the second inaugural calling for the binding up of the nation's wounds with malice toward none and charity for all. With these words Lincoln invoked the New Testament lesson of forgiveness; he urged a soft peace once the war was over. But although he believed in a soft peace, it could be won only by a hard war. This was an Old Testament concept, and for Lincoln's Old Testament vision of a hard war, listen to *these* words from the second inaugural: "American Slavery is one of those offences which, in the providence of God . . . He now wills to remove [through] this terrible war, as the woe due to those by whom the offence came. . . . Fondly do we hope—fervently do we pray—that this mighty scourge of war may speedily pass away. Yet if God wills that it continue, until all the wealth piled by the bondman's two hundred and fifty years of unrequited toil shall be sunk, and until every drop of blood drawn with the lash, shall be paid by another drawn with the sword, as was said three thousand years ago, so still it must be said 'the judgments of the Lord, are true and righteous altogether.' "[19]

This was the language not only of the Old Testament, but also of revolution. In the second respect in which the Civil War has been viewed as a revolution—its effecting the abolition of slavery—Lincoln fits the pattern of a revolutionary leader. He was a reluctant one at first, to be sure, but in the end he was more radical than Washington or Jefferson or any of the leaders of the first revolution, who led a successful struggle for independence from Britain but did not accomplish a fundamental change in the society they led. Lincoln did preside over such a fundamental change. Indeed, as he put it himself, also in the second inaugural, neither side had anticipated such "fundamental and astounding" changes when the war began.

THESE WORDS introduce the third respect in which the Civil War can be viewed as a revolution: it destroyed not only slavery but also the social structure of the old South which had been founded on slavery, and it radically altered the power balance between the North and the South. It changed the fundamental direction of American development. As Mark Twain and Charles Dudley Warner described it in their classic novel published in 1873, *The Gilded Age,* which furnished a name for the postwar era, the Civil War had "uprooted institutions that were centuries old, changed the politics of a people, transformed the social life of half the country, and wrought so profoundly upon the entire national character that the influence cannot be measured short of two or three generations."[20]

These were the kinds of changes that caused the notable American historian Charles Beard to describe the Civil War as "the second American Revolution, and in a strict sense, the First"—because the Revolution of 1776 had not produced fundamental changes in the social structure, while the Revolution of 1861, that "social cataclysm in which the capitalists, laborers, and farmers of the North and West drove from power in the national government the planting aristocracy of the South," had brought forth "the unquestioned establishment of a new power in the government, making vast changes in the arrangement of classes, in the distribution of wealth, in the course of industrial development."[21]

What were some of these vast, revolutionary changes? First, a transformation in political power relations between the North and the South. Before the Civil War the slave states, despite having a declining percentage of the population, had used their domination of the Jeffersonian party and then the Jacksonian Democratic party to achieve an extraordinary degree of power in the national government. In 1861 the United States had been living under the Constitution for seventy-two years. During forty-nine of those years—or two-thirds of the time—the president had been a Southerner and a slaveholder. After the Civil War a century passed before another Southerner was elected president. In Congress, twenty-three out of the thirty-six Speakers of the House and twenty-four of the thirty-six presidents pro tem of the Senate down to 1861 were from the South—again, two-thirds of the total. For a half century after the war, *none* of the speakers or presidents pro tem was from the South. Before the war, twenty of the thirty-five Supreme Court justices had been from the South; during the next half century, only five of the twenty-six justices appointed to the Court were Southerners.

The sweeping transformation in the economic balance between North and South was no less revolutionary than these changes in political power. During the decade of the 1860s the total of northern wealth, as measured by property and capital, increased by 50 percent while the total of southern wealth *decreased* by 60 percent. In 1861 the South's share of the national wealth had been 30 percent, about equal to its percentage of the population; in 1870 the South's share of the national wealth was only 12 percent. In 1860 the average per capita income of all Southerners, black and white, was two-thirds of the northern average; after the war the southern average dropped to less than two-fifths of the northern average and did not rise above that level for the rest of the nineteenth century. The output of southern industry in proportion to that of the North was cut in half by the war; the value of southern agricultural land in relation to that of the North was cut by three-quarters.[22]

These changes occurred because when the Civil War became a total war, the invading army intentionally destroyed the economic capacity of the South to wage war. Union armies ripped up thousands of miles of southern railroads and blew up hundreds of bridges. More than half of the South's farm machinery was destroyed by the war, two-fifths of its livestock was killed, and one-quarter of its white males of military age—also the prime age for economic production—was killed, a higher proportion than suffered by any European power in World War I, that holocaust that ravaged a continent and spread revolution through many of its countries.

Union Generals William Tecumseh Sherman and Philip Sheridan saw more clearly than anyone else the nature of modern, total war, a war between peoples rather than simply between armies, a war in which the fighting left nothing untouched or unchanged. "We are not only fighting hostile armies, but a hostile people," wrote Sherman in the middle of the war. "We cannot change the hearts of those people of the South," he said in 1864 as his army began its march from Atlanta to the sea, "but we can make war so terrible . . . [and] make them so sick of war that generations would pass away before they would again appeal to it."[23] While Sherman's army was marching through Georgia and South Carolina destroying everything in its path, Sheridan's army cut a similar swath through the Shenandoah Valley making sure that it, like Georgia and South Carolina, would produce no more food or munitions for Confederate forces.

Although Abraham Lincoln was a compassionate man who deplored this destruction and suffering, he nevertheless sanctioned it as the only way to win the war. After all, he had told Southerners two years earlier that the North did not intend to fight with elder-stalk squirts and rose water. He had warned them that the longer they fought, the more eggs would be broken. Now, in 1864, he officially conveyed to Sheridan the "thanks of the nation, and my own personal admiration and gratitude, for [your] operations in the Shenandoah Valley"; he sent Sherman and his army "grateful acknowledgments" for their march through Georgia. In early 1865 Lincoln delightedly described the military situation to a visitor with a typical Lincolnian metaphor: General Grant, he said, "has the bear by the hind leg, while Sherman takes off its hide."[24]

The second American Revolution, as Charles Beard viewed it, involved not only this destruction of the southern plantation aristocracy but also the consolidation of the northern entrepreneurial capitalist class in national power, supported by its urban and rural middle-class allies. Legislation passed by northern wartime congresses promoted this development. The Republican party had inherited from its Hamiltonian and Whig forbears a commitment to the use of government to foster economic development through tariffs to protect industry, a centralized and regulated banking system, investment subsidies and land grants to high-risk but socially beneficial transportation enterprises, and government support for education. By 1860 the Republican party had also pledged itself to homestead legislation to provide farmers with an infusion of capital in the form of free land. Before 1860, the southern-dominated Democratic party that controlled the federal government had repeatedly defeated or frustrated these measures: the Democrats lowered the tariff, abolished the Second Bank of the United States, and blocked land-grant legislation for the building of a transcontinental railroad; a Democratic president vetoed a homestead act in 1860 and also vetoed another act granting public lands to the states for the establishment of colleges for agricultural education. The withdrawal of Southerners from Congress when their states seceded gave northern Republicans firm control of Congress. They used this power to pass the legislation previously blocked by Democrats: a higher tariff in 1861; a homestead act; a land-grant college act; a Pacific railroad act providing loans and land grants for a transcontinental railroad in 1862; and a national banking act in 1863, which, along with the legal tender act of the previous year authorizing the issuance of a federal currency, the famous greenbacks, gave the national government effective control over the nation's monetary system for the first time. In addition, to finance the war the government had marketed huge bond issues to the public and passed an internal revenue act which imposed a large array of federal taxes for the first time, including a progressive income tax.

This astonishing blitz of laws, most of them passed within a span of less than one year, did more to reshape the relation of the government to the economy than any comparable effort except perhaps the first hundred days of the New Deal. This Civil War legislation, in the words of one historian, created a "blueprint for modern America." It helped promote what another scholar termed "the last capitalist revolution" whereby the Civil War destroyed the "older social structure of planta-tion slavery" and installed "competitive democratic capitalism" in un-challenged domination of the American economy and polity. That this capitalism itself became a form of entrenched conservatism exploiting labor and resisting change a generation or two later does not nullify the revolutionary meaning of its triumph over the slave South and planta-tion agriculture in the 1860s. And as a lifelong Whig who had favored these measures to promote banking, transportation, and industry as a means of bringing a higher standard of living to all Americans, and who believed that the abolition of slave labor would enhance the dig-nity and value of *free* labor, Abraham Lincoln was one of the principal architects of this capitalist revolution which, to quote Charles Beard again, made "vast changes in the arrangement of classes, in the distribu-tion of wealth, in the course of industrial development."[25]

WHAT conclusions can we draw, then, that make sense of those con-trasting pictures of Lincoln the conservative and Lincoln the revolu-tionary that I quoted at the beginning of this lecture? Although it may seem like a contradiction in terms, I think it appropriate to describe Lincoln as a conservative revolutionary. That is, he wanted to conserve the Union as the revolutionary heritage of the founding fathers. Pre-serving this heritage was the *purpose* of the war; all else became a means to achieve this end. As Lincoln phrased it in his famous public letter to Horace Greeley in August 1862, "My paramount object in this struggle *is* to save the Union, and is *not* either to save or to destroy slavery. . . . What I do about slavery and the colored race, I do because I believe it helps to save the Union."[26] By the time he wrote these words, Lincoln had pretty well made up his mind that to save the Union he must destroy slavery. The means always remained subordinated to the end, but the means did become as essential to the northern war effort as the end itself. In that sense perhaps we could describe Lincoln as a prag-matic revolutionary, for as a pragmatist he adapted the means to the end. Thus we can agree with the historian Norman Graebner, whom I quoted earlier as stating that Lincoln "accepted the need of dealing with things as they were, not as he would have wished them to be." But instead of concluding, as Graebner did, that this made Lincoln a con-servative, I conclude that it made him a revolutionary. He was not an ideological revolutionary, to be sure—Lincoln was no Robespierre or

Lenin with a blueprint for a new order—but he was a pragmatic revolutionary who found it necessary to destroy slavery and create a new birth of freedom in order to preserve the Union.

"The dogmas of the quiet past," Lincoln told Congress in December 1862, "are inadequate to the stormy present. As our case is new, we must think anew, and act anew." It was *the war itself*, not the ideological blueprints of Lincoln or any other leader, that generated the radical momentum that made it a second American Revolution. Like most wars that become total wars, the Civil War snowballed into huge and unanticipated dimensions and took on a life and purpose of its own far beyond the causes that had started it. As Lincoln said in his second inaugural, neither side "expected for the war the magnitude or the duration which it has already attained" or anticipated results so "fundamental and astounding." Or as he put it on another occasion, "I claim not to have controlled events, but confess plainly that events have controlled me."[27] But in conceding that the war rather than he had shaped the thrust and direction of the revolution, Lincoln was perhaps too modest. For it was his own superb leadership, strategy, and sense of timing as president, commander-in-chief, and head of the Republican party that determined the pace of the revolution and insured its success. With a less able man as president and commander-in-chief, the North might have lost the war or ended it under the leadership of Democrats who would have given its outcome a very different shape. Thus in accepting "the need of dealing with things as they were," Lincoln became not a conservative statesman but a revolutionary statesman.

NOTES

1 / James G. Randall, *Lincoln the Liberal Statesman* (New York, 1947), 178, 177; *The Collected Works of Abraham Lincoln*, ed. Roy C. Basler, Marion Delores Pratt, and Lloyd A. Dunlap, 9 vols. (New Brunswick, N.J., 1953–55), 2:272, 273.

2 / T. Harry Williams, "Lincoln and the Radicals," in *Grant, Lee, Lincoln and the Radicals: Essays on Civil War Leadership*, ed. Grady McWhiney (Evanston, Ill., 1964), 114; Norman A. Graebner, "Abraham Lincoln: Conservative Statesman," in *The Enduring Lincoln*, ed. Graebner (Urbana, Ill., 1959), 68.

3 / Georges Clemenceau, *American Reconstruction, 1865–1870*, ed. Fernand Balensperger, trans. Margaret MacVeagh (New York, 1926), 294; Disraeli, quoted in Belle Becker Sideman and Lillian Friedman, eds., *Europe Looks at the Civil War* (New York, 1960), 233.

4 / *Springfield Republican,* September 24, 1862; Otto Olsen, "Abraham Lincoln as Revolutionary," *Civil War History* 24 (1978): 213–24.

5 / *Collected Works of Lincoln,* 1:278, 438; 2:115, 130; Saul K. Padover, ed. and trans., *Karl Marx on America and the Civil War* (New York, 1972), 237, 263, 264.

6 / All three quotations are from James Oakes, *The Ruling Race: A History of American Slaveholders* (New York, 1982), 239–40.

7 / Ibid., 240.

8 / Yancey, quoted in George M. Fredrickson, *The Black Image in the White Mind: The Debate on Afro-American Character and Destiny, 1817–1914* (New York, 1971), 61; *The Works of John C. Calhoun,* ed. Richard K. Crallé, 6 vols. (New York, 1854–57), 4:505–6.

9 / *Atlanta Daily Intelligencer,* December 13, 1860.

10 / *New York Tribune,* May 21, 1862; *Collected Works of Lincoln,* 7:301–2; 4:160.

11 / *Collected Works of Lincoln,* 4:434 n.

12 / Tyler Dennett, ed., *Lincoln and the Civil War in the Diaries and Letters of John Hay* (New York, 1939), 19; *Collected Works of Lincoln,* 4:439, 438; 5:53.

13 / Moncure Conway, *The Rejected Stone: or Insurrection vs. Resurrection in America* (Boston, 1861), 75–80, 110; *Principia,* May 4, 1861; *Congressional Globe,* 37th Cong., 1st sess., 414; Margaret Shortreed, "The Anti-Slavery Radicals: From Crusade to Revolution 1840–1868," *Past and Present,* no. 16, November 1959, p. 77.

14 / *Collected Works of Lincoln,* 5:49; 7:281.

15 / Ibid., 5:144–46, 222–23, 317–19; *New York Tribune,* July 19, 1862; Gideon Welles, "The History of Emancipation," *Galaxy* 14 (1872): 842–43.

16 / Allan Nevins, *The War for the Union: War Becomes Revolution* (New York, 1960), 239; *War of the Rebellion: Official Records of the Union and Confederate Armies,* ser. 1, vol. 24, pt. 3, p. 157; General Grenville Dodge, quoted in Bruce Catton, *Grant Moves South* (Boston, 1960), 294.

17 / *Collected Works of Lincoln,* 6:149–50, 408–9.

18 / Ibid., 5:346, 350; Welles, "History of Emancipation," 842–43.

19 / *Collected Works of Lincoln,* 8:333.

20 / Mark Twain and Charles Dudley Warner, *The Gilded Age,* New American Library ed. (New York, 1969), 137–38.

21 / Charles A. Beard and Mary R. Beard, *The Rise of American Civilization,* 2 vols. (New York, 1927), 2:53–54.

22 / These data are drawn from the following sources: James L. Sellers, "The Economic Incidence of the Civil War in the South," *Mississippi Valley Historical Review* 14 (1927): 179–91; Stanley Engerman, "Some Economic Factors in Southern Backwardness in the Nineteenth Century," in *Essays in Regional Economics,* ed. John F. Kain and John R. Meyers (Cambridge, Mass., 1971), 300–302; Claudia D. Goldin and Frank D. Lewis, "The Economic Cost of the American Civil War: Estimates and Implications," *Journal of Economic History* 35 (1975): 299–326; Lee Soltow, *Men and Wealth in the United States 1850–1870* (New Haven, 1975); Donald B. Dodd and Wynelle S. Dodd, comps., *Historical Statistics of the South 1790–1970* (University, Ala., 1973).

23 / John Bennett Walters, "General William T. Sherman and Total War," *Journal of Southern History* 14 (1948): 463, 470.

24 / *Collected Works of Lincoln,* 8:73–74, 182; Burke Davis, *Sherman's March* (New York, 1980), 140.

25 / Leonard P. Curry, *Blueprint for Modern America: Nonmilitary Legislation of the First*

Civil War Congress (Nashville, Tenn., 1968); Barrington Moore, Jr., *Social Origins of Dictatorship and Democracy: Lord and Peasant in the Making of the Modern World* (Boston, 1966), 111–55 on the American Civil War as the "last capitalist revolution"; Gabor S. Boritt, *Lincoln and the Economics of the American Dream* (Memphis, Tenn., 1978).

26 / *Collected Works of Lincoln,* 5:388.

27 / Ibid., 8:332–33; 7:282.

DON E. FEHRENBACHER taught at Stanford University for thirty-one years and became William Robertson Coe Professor of History and American Studies Emeritus in 1984. Fehrenbacher has been an NEH fellow, a Guggenheim fellow (twice), and, in 1985–86, a visiting fellow at the Huntington Library. He is the author of several books and numerous essays on Lincoln, and his book *The Dred Scott Case: Its Significance in American Law and Politics* won the Pulitzer Prize in History in 1979.

WILLIAM E. GIENAPP is associate professor of History at the University of Wyoming, Laramie. He is the author of *The Origins of the Republican Party, 1852–1856*, which will be published by Oxford University Press in 1986.

MICHAEL F. HOLT is professor of History at the University of Virginia. He is author of *Forging a Majority: The Formation of the Republican Party in Pittsburgh, 1848–1860* and *The Political Crisis of the 1850s*.

JAMES M. MC PHERSON is Edwards Professor of American History at Princeton University. He has written five books and been the co-author of two. In 1965 he received the Anisfield-Wolf Award in race relations for his *The Struggle for Equality: Abolitionists and the Negro in the Civil War and Reconstruction*. His most recent book is *Ordeal By Fire: The Civil War and Reconstruction*. He is currently completing a volume in the *Oxford History of the United States*, tentatively entitled *This Mighty Scourge of War: From Guadalupe Hidalgo to Appomattox*.

STEPHEN B. OATES, Paul Murray Kendall Professor of Biography at the University of Massachusetts, Amherst, has published twelve books, including *With Malice toward None: The Life of Abraham Lincoln* (1977), *Our Fiery Trial: Abraham Lincoln, John Brown, and the Civil War Era* (1979), and *Abraham Lincoln: The Man behind the Myths* (1984). *With Malice toward None,* which has appeared in several languages, won a Christopher Award for "affirming the highest values of the human spirit, artistic and technical proficiency, and significant degree of public acceptance," and the Barondess/Lincoln Award of the New York Civil War Round Table. His *Let the Trumpet Sound: The Life of Martin Luther King, Jr.* (1982), also won a Christopher Award, as well as the Robert F. Kennedy Memorial Book Award.

JOHN L. THOMAS is George L. Littlefield Professor of American History at Brown University. His most recent work is *Alternative America: Henry George, Edward Bellamy, Henry Demarest Lloyd, and the Adversary Tradition.*

ROBERT H. WIEBE, professor of History at Northwestern University, has general interests in American history. His works include *The Search for Order: 1877–1920, The Segmented Society,* and, most recently, *The Opening of American Society: From the Adoption of the Constitution to the Eve of Civil War.*